# THE PILLARS OF MARRIAGE

## H. Norman Wright

**Regal Books**

A Division of GL Publications
Ventura, California, U.S.A.

**Other Books by H. Norman Wright**
*Communication: Key to Your Marriage*
*Preparing for Parenthood*
*Seasons of a Marriage*
*More Communication Keys for Your Marriage*
*So You're Getting Married*

Published by Regal Books
A Division of GL Publications
Ventura, California 93006
Printed in U.S.A.

Scripture quotations in this publication are from the following versions:
*NASB:* *New American Standard Bible.* © The Lockman Foundation 1960, 1962, 1963, 1968, 1971, 1972, 1973, 1975. Used by permission.
*AMP:* *AMPLIFIED BIBLE, The.* Copyright © 1962, 1964, 1965 by Zondervan Publishing House. Used by permission.
*TLB:* *The Living Bible,* Copyright © 1971 by Tyndale House Publishers, Wheaton, Illinois. Used by permission.
*Phillips:* *THE NEW TESTAMENT IN MODERN ENGLISH,* Revised Edition, J.B. Phillips, Translator. © J.B. Phillips 1958, 1960, 1972. Used by permission of Macmillan Publishing Co., Inc.
*RSV:* *Revised Standard Version* of the Bible, copyrighted 1946 and 1952 by the Division of Christian Education of the NCCC, U.S.A., and used by permission.
*NEB:* *The New English Bible.* © The Delegates of the Oxford University Press and The Syndics of the Cambridge University Press 1961, 1970. Reprinted by permission.
*MLB:* *MODERN LANGUAGE BIBLE. The Berkeley Version.* Copyright © 1945, 1959, 1969, 1971 by Zondervan Publishing House. Used by permission.
*KJV:* *The Authorized King James Version.*

Library of Congress Catalog Card No. 78-68849
ISBN 0-8307-0698-4

**9 10 11 12 13 14 15 / 91 90 89 88 87**

Rights for publishing this book in other languages are contracted by Gospel Literature International (GLINT) foundation. GLINT also provides technical help for the adaptation, translation, and publishing of Bible study resources and books in scores of languages worldwide. For further information, contact GLINT, Post Office Box 488, Rosemead, California, 91770, U.S.A., or the publisher.

# CONTENTS

A Leader's Guide for use with this book
is available from your church supplier.

## CHAPTER ONE

# LOOKING AT MARRIAGE

When we arrive at the doctor's office, we are first examined to discover if anything is amiss in our physical being. Our eyes, ears, nose, throat, and pulse are checked. We step on the scales to be weighed, and often we groan! (Sometimes the scales groan too!) The doctor examines us thoroughly and in most cases states: "You're all right."

In other cases he recommends medication or rest. In a few of us he may discover a major disease eating away which, if left untreated, would eventually destroy us. In this case he may have to operate and literally cut away that insidious growth that is draining us of energy and life. But after the operation there is recovery, health, and well-being. And following the operation many experience better health than they had for many years.

As you read this book your marital relationship will undergo a visit to the marital practitioner instead of the physician. Medicine sometimes tastes bitter, and recovery from an operation is often painful. The "medicine" prescribed here may taste bitter too, and the "surgery" your marriage may undergo could be painful. But that's all right, because marital health and an enriched marriage are the prognosis.

That's quite an expectation to ask from a book. Actually a book will never bring about change, but you can. As you and your mate read, think, discuss, evaluate, apply, and plan—change can occur.

At the start of this book we are going to put your marriage under a microscope. In a way this could be the most uncomfortable chapter in the entire book. You may see yourself and your spouse in this chapter and begin to squirm. But that's all right. This book is designed to help individuals and couples change *in a positive manner.*

One of the reasons for proceeding in this manner is to help resolve one of my own frustrations. As a marriage counselor I see many Christian couples who have chosen to live in pain, dissatisfaction, and disharmony for many years. Why they choose this path instead of taking affirmative action will always remain somewhat of a mystery to me! Why not take positive steps even if pain is involved? Marriage has the potential for some of the greatest joy in life as well as the greatest pain.

While preparing to write this book I went to Christian and secular bookstores to scan through the dozens of books on marriage. I found that few of the topics I wanted to present in this book were discussed in books currently available. These topics were selected from the suggestions of hundreds of couples in Sunday School classes, in marriage enrichment seminars, and in counseling.

What is marriage? You have your own thoughts and beliefs about marriage. Let's consider them now.

**WHAT DO YOU THINK?**

Here are several questions for you to answer. Both you and your spouse should answer each question individually without consulting each other.

I. If you had to explain marriage to another person, what would you say?

2. What do you feel are the ingredients of a successful or fulfilling marriage?

3. What needs did God intend a marriage to fulfill? List at least five.

4. Think back now to the days of your courtship. What month and year did you meet your mate?

5. Where did you meet, and what was your first impression?

6. What were you thinking the first time you kissed your spouse?

7. In what way did you think your spouse was similar to you before you married?

8. Do you have a five-year plan for the development of your marriage?

9. When was the last time you told your spouse that you love him/her?

10. List six loving acts you performed toward your spouse in the last month.

11. List six loving acts your spouse performed toward you in the last month.

12. When was the last time you gave your spouse a compliment you had never given him/her before?

13. What three words would you use to describe your marriage at the present time?

---

Now that you've had a chance to think about your marriage, let me share some thoughts about marriage. Marriage is a journey that involves the selection of numerous paths. Each path has its own characteristics and destinations, some good and some not. Marriage is a cooperative venture in which two people are developing a oneness at the same time they are maintaining and enhancing their own individuality and potential.

A Christian marriage is a commitment involving three individuals—husband, wife, and Jesus Christ. It is a pledge of mutual fidelity and mutual submission.

Marriage is also one of God's greatest schools of learning, for it can be a place where a husband and wife are refined. The rough edges are gradually filed away until there is a greater and smoother working and blending together, and both individuals are fulfilled.

God intended a Christian marriage to fulfill individual needs. John Lavender, in his excellent book *Your Marriage*

*Needs Three Love Affairs,* cited seven needs from the Word of God that a Christian marriage is designed to meet.[1]

In Genesis 2:18 and 24 God says, "It is not good for the man to be alone; I will make him a helper suitable for him. . . . For this cause a man shall leave his father and his mother, and shall cleave to his wife; and they shall become one flesh." From this passage we understand that marriage brings about *completion.* Marriage involves a mysterious merging of two separate but equal individuals in such a way that they learn to complement each other and thereby actually complete each other.

We need to remember that the word here is "completion," not "competition." Completion means that fellowship is involved, companionship is involved, but most of all, completion involves friendship.

A friend is a person with whom you feel comfortable. A friend is an individual whose company you prefer over another's. This type of person is someone you can count on—not just for support and encouragement but for out-and-out honesty.

A true friend is an individual who believes in you. He/she shares some of the same beliefs about your potential, your dreams, your concerns. You want to spend all of your life with him/her.

A friend is someone who fulfills Galatians 6:2: "Bear one another's burdens." When you hurt, your friend hurts. When you share your concerns and your hurts with him/her, the pain is eased. A friend is someone who gives you safety and trust. You know that what you share will stop right there. It will never be used against you.

Laughter is a part of friendship, but laughter with you, not at you. Praying is a part of friendship too—praying for each other and praying with each other.

A friend is an individual with whom you can share your ideas, your beliefs, and your philosophies; and you can grow

9

together intellectually. This does not mean that you have the same level of intelligence or the same educational background, but you find a similarity between you, and you share it together. A friend is one who stands by you in a time of difficulty and trouble, while maintaining a level of objectivity.

Another way of describing a friend is to say that he/she is a person with whom you can be yourself. You can be totally exposed and open. A friend is someone who can see you at your worst as well as at your best, and still love you just the same.

Are you experiencing this kind of relationship at the present time in your marriage relationship? Could this area of your life be improved? Completion is a process, but it does take work and effort.

A second need that is fulfilled in marriage is *consolation.* Genesis 2:18 states: "I will make him a helper suitable for him." Consolation comes from speaking in a manner that encourages, supports, and brings about feeling to the other person. A married individual has the opportunity of being used by God as a channel of His healing grace.

Proverbs puts it this way in chapter 12, verse 25: "Anxiety in the heart of a man weighs it down, but a good word makes it glad." Proverbs 25:11 says, "A word fitly spoken and in due season is like apples of gold in a setting of silver" (*AMP*).

God also designed Christian marriage for *communication.* Communication is the means by which one person has the opportunity of learning to know and understand his/her mate. David and Vera Mace likened communication to "a large house with many rooms to which a couple fall heir on their wedding day. Their hope is to use and enjoy these rooms, as we do the rooms in a comfortable home, so that they will serve the many activities that make up their shared life. But in many marriages doors are found to be locked—they represent areas in the relationship that the couple are unable to explore together. Attempts to open these doors lead to failure and

10

frustration. The right key cannot be found. So the couple resigns themselves to living together in only a few rooms which can be opened easily, leaving the rest of the house with all its promising possibilities unexplored and unused. There is, however, a master key that will open every door. It is not easy to find. Or, more correctly, it has to be forged by the couple together, and this can be very difficult. It is the great art of effective marital communication."[2]

Yet another need that is fulfilled in marriage is *coition* or sexual fulfillment. Sexuality is our celebration of God's continuing creativity. God chose to demonstrate His creative activity in conception of new persons through the intimate act of love union. He has honored the simple act of joining bodies with the ultimate significance of beginning life.

Two who give themselves to each other in the intimacy of marriage celebrate the eternal potential of their act of love. This awareness of its creative meaning gives character to sexual union, even when it is meant as an act of joyous communion with no intention of conception. Then, too, it is a celebration of His creation.[3]

In your marriage relationship, how do you feel about sexuality? Is it joyful and fulfilling? Or is it more of a burden and a nuisance? God is the author of sexuality, and He considers it "very good" (Gen. 1:31). As a couple, have you taken the opportunity to pray together, thanking God for the uniqueness of your bodies? Have you thanked Him for the perfect design that He has given to each of you and praised Him for sexuality itself?

Consider the words that Harry Hollis, Jr., wrote in his excellent book *Thank God for Sex:* [4]

*Lord, it's hard to know what sex really is—*
*Is it some demon put here to torment me?*
*Or some delicious seducer from reality?*
*It is neither of these, Lord.*

11

*I know what sex is—*
  *It is body and spirit,*
  *It is strong embrace and gentle hand-holding,*
  *It is open nakedness and hidden mystery,*
  *It is joyful tears on honeymoon faces, and*
  *It is tears on wrinkled faces at a golden wedding*
    *anniversary.*

*Sex is a quiet look across the room,*
  *a love note on a pillow,*
  *a rose laid on a breakfast plate,*
  *laughter in the night.*

*Sex is life—not all of life—*
  *but wrapped up in the meaning of life.*

*Sex is your good gift, O God,*
  *To enrich life,*
  *To continue the race,*
  *To communicate,*
  *To show me who I am,*
  *To reveal my mate,*
  *To cleanse through "one flesh."*

*Lord, some people say sex and religion don't mix;*
  *But your Word says sex is good.*

*Help me to keep it good in my life.*
*Help me to be open about sex*
  *And still protect its mystery.*
*Help me to see that sex*
  *Is neither demon nor deity.*
*Help me not to climb into a fantasy world*
  *Of imaginary sexual partners;*
*Keep me in the real world*
  *To love the people you have created.*

*Teach me that my soul does not have to frown at sex*
  *for me to be a Christian.*

*It's hard for many people to say, "Thank God for sex!"*
  *Because for them sex is more a problem than a gift.*
*They need to know that sex and gospel*
  *Can be linked together again.*
*They need to hear the good news about sex.*
*Show me how I can help them.*

*Thank you, Lord, for making me a sexual being.*
*Thank you for showing me how to treat others with*
  *trust and love.*
*Thank you for letting me talk to you about sex.*
*Thank you that I feel free to say:*
  *"Thank God for sex!"*

Another need that can be satisfied within marriage is *creation,* bringing a new life into being. Dr. Lavender put it this way: "When you and your mate give yourselves to each other in the intimacy of Christian marriage, you not only celebrate your oneness in Spirit, but by the simple act of joining bodies, become participants of God in the continuum of life."[5]

Another purpose for marriage is *correlation.* Correlation has to do with the relationships that exist in a Christian home. Unfortunately in many marriages we have instead of a Christian home, a home full of Christians.

The husband and wife relationship or the family life is a microcosm of the Body of Christ, or a little church. It is a fellowship of believers together. This relationship, particularly between husband and wife, should reflect to others—the non-Christian community—what a church is really like. A marriage or a family should be a church in miniature.

"Speaking the truth in love, we are to grow up in all aspects into Him, who is the head, even Christ, from whom the whole body, being fitted and held together by that which every joint supplies, according to the proper working of each individual part, causes the growth of the body for the building up of itself in love" (Eph. 4:15,16, *NASB* ).

The final need that is fulfilled in marriage is *Christianization.* A Christian family can be one of the most powerful and persuasive evangelistic forces on earth. However, many Christian marriages do not reflect the reality of the presence of Christ. Living the Christian life in a family is difficult, but it has a far greater effect upon the world than preaching or the distribution of tracts. The Christian family, in a sense, is a proof of the reality of the power of God in an individual's life.

Often these needs, which God intended to be met in marriage, are not met. Sociologists John F. Cuber and Peggy Haroff have suggested five different categories of marriage which may help explain why plans, dreams, and purposes go astray.[6] They are presented here with some additional aspects of the relationship described.

The first type of marriage, called the *devitalized marriage,* is a placid, half-alive relationship. This marriage is devoid of emotional involvement, so there is neither conflict nor passion. Individuals in this marriage can be thought of as "married singles." They both live as separate a life as possible and still remain married.

The husband provides his wife with money for running the household and leaves the details of that to her. His time is consumed with his work and hobbies. There is very little bother from his wife concerning the children or the house unless absolutely necessary. Their communication is definitely surface level with no sharing of thoughts *or* feelings. Sexual relationships are routine and almost obligatory. This type of married life is almost an exchange of services. Bed and board are shared, and that's it!

Even marriages that have previously developed into a positive relationship can slip into this style. Many replacements crop up to impede the relationship. Work can be one, especially if the husband is using his performance and involvement at work to enhance his self-concept. The newspaper, television, sports, reading, children, recreation, hobbies, and church are activities that are innocent in themselves but that can be used as escape avenues, which characterize this style of marriage.

Diagram 1 shows a visual way of depicting this kind of marriage.

DIAGRAM 1

**DEVITALIZED MARRIAGE**

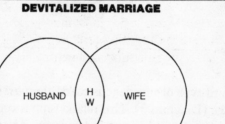

LEVEL OF INVOLVEMENT

A second type of marriage is called the *conflict-habitu-ated marriage* (Diagram 2). The couple is fighting constantly but amazingly enough seems to enjoy it and can't seem to live without it! Often couples like this are referred to as "weary wranglers." Over the years they have developed finesse in their ability to strike out and hurt. They find themselves in a dilemma. They know their methods are basically destructive but seem unable to change.

In some cases they find a sense of comfort in being hostile to each other, because then they can blame the other person for their unhappiness. Aggression can either be direct outbursts or subtle forays. Fresh wounds are inflicted before the previous ones have had time to develop protective scabs. The relationship is volatile, but both seem to thrive on it. The involvement level is greater in this marriage but painful.

DIAGRAM 2

## CONFLICT-HABITUATED MARRIAGE

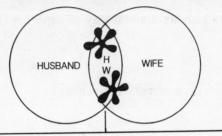

LEVEL OF INVOLVEMENT

A third type of marriage is called the *passive-congenial* marriage (Diagram 3). This relationship is comfortable and has very few ups and downs. In some ways it is quite similar to the first style but with slightly more involvement. However, the involvement is not very exciting, and once certain routines and habits have been established, they vary little. A humdrum routine sets in and lasts for many years.

DIAGRAM 3

## PASSIVE-CONGENIAL MARRIAGE

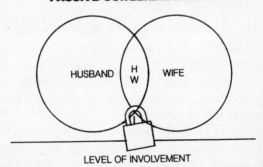

LEVEL OF INVOLVEMENT

A fourth type of marriage is the *total marriage*. It is characterized by constant togetherness and mutual interest. Every experience of life is shared with each other, and little or nothing is conducted separately. The relationship is very intense because of the closeness, but it is also fragile. Any minor change or alteration can rock the boat.

Individual growth is limited because the relationship is everything, which creates a degree of smothering and stifling. Often this marriage is held out to be the ideal because "they are so close and do everything together!" In time, one or both may feel constricted and boxed-in because attempts to change on their part may meet with an onslaught of resistance.

Even when suggested changes are positive and beneficial, efforts are blocked. Any change upsets the precious and delicate equilibrium that has been established.

Another title for this marriage is the *eggshell relationship*. One false step and "crunch" goes the relationship. This marriage is depicted in Diagram 4.

DIAGRAM 4

**TOTAL MARRIAGE**

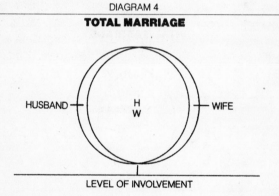

HUSBAND — WIFE

H
W

LEVEL OF INVOLVEMENT

A final type of marriage is the *vital marriage*. Each person is very involved in the other's interests, but they are not locked into the restrictions of the "total" marriage. In this marriage the couple likes to do things together whenever possible and, as much as possible, they share all roles within the marriage. They are not locked into stereotyped roles for male and female. Thoughts and feelings are open to each other and communication is extensive between the two.

17

The honesty that is so vital in building a marriage is present. David and Vera Mace described the importance of honesty: "Because marriage is a relationship of shared intimacy, it requires a level of honesty between the partners that goes much deeper than conventional social relationships. People cannot truly share life without knowing each other, and they cannot know each other unless their thoughts are open to each other to a degree that happens in few other human relationships. To be secretive or reserved or defensive toward each other in marriage is inevitably to condemn the relationship to superficiality."[7]

Much of the marriage is together, but each has maintained his own individuality and uniqueness. Diagram 5 pictures this type of marriage.

DIAGRAM 5

**VITAL MARRIAGE**

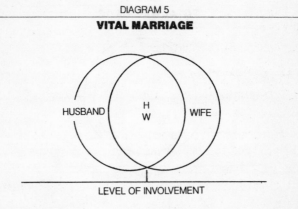

LEVEL OF INVOLVEMENT

Husband and wife cooperate in running the home, rearing the children, managing finances, and making decisions. They face and work through disagreements and the spouses are supportive to each other. This marriage usually contains reasonably well-adjusted people who are willing to take the risk of making changes to enhance and enrich their marriage. They are similar to a pair of porcupines.

"Imagine a group of porcupines settling down to sleep on a cold winter night. Being warm-blooded creatures, they huddle together in search of mutual warmth. But the point inevitably is reached when sharp quills prick tender flesh, and they recoil away from each other. In this fashion they shuffle sleepily back and forth, back and forth, until they find a point of equilibrium at which they derive the maximum possible amount of warmth from each other, consistent with not pricking each other!

"The porcupines illustrate very well the process by which two married people achieve a close relationship. We could call it mutual adaptation. It means strengthening the affinities and resolving, as far as possible, the hostilities. It is a difficult art calling for skill and patience. But it can be learned; and those who learn it have in their hands the means to raise their involvement with each other as marriage partners to the highest level of which they as a couple are capable, without violating the sanctity of each other's personhood."[8]

## WHAT DO YOU THINK?

Let's take a look at the progression of your marital relationship. Thinking back on the five types of marriage, consider your marital past and present. Remember that some elements of each type may be seen in your marriage. These categories are not rigid; they often overlap.

1. On the graph below, circle the point opposite the type of marriage that best describes your marital relationship during each year of your marriage. Then connect the circles in chronological order and trace your marital pattern from left to right across the graph. You may find that the curve slopes upward, indicating an improvement in your marriage relationship. You may find a downward slope, indicating deterioration. Or you may may find that your points, when connected, form a line that goes up and down or stays about level all the way across the graph.

| CATEGORY | YEARS MARRIED | | | | | | | | | | | | | |
| --- | --- | --- | --- | --- | --- | --- | --- | --- | --- | --- | --- | --- | --- | --- |
| | 1 | 2 | 4 | 6 | 8 | 10 | 12 | 14 | 16 | 18 | 20 | 22 | 24 | 26 |
| Vital | ● | ● | ● | ● | ● | ● | ● | ● | ● | ● | ● | ● | ● | ● |
| Total | ● | ● | ● | ● | ● | ● | ● | ● | ● | ● | ● | ● | ● | ● |
| Passive-congenial | ● | ● | ● | ● | ● | ● | ● | ● | ● | ● | ● | ● | ● | ● |
| Conflict-habituated | ● | ● | ● | ● | ● | ● | ● | ● | ● | ● | ● | ● | ● | ● |
| Devitalized | ● | ● | ● | ● | ● | ● | ● | ● | ● | ● | ● | ● | ● | ● |

DIAGRAM 6

2. What did you do to cause your marriage to improve or deteriorate?

3. What did your spouse do to cause your marriage to improve or deteriorate?

4. If your marriage was in any of the first four categories, what did you do to bring the marriage there or keep it there?

5. What did your spouse do to bring your marriage there or keep it there?

6. What is your plan? Unless you have goals and plans, little is accomplished. Looking at your marriage at the present time, what do you feel needs to be done to move it toward the "vital relationship" or keep it there?

7. List specific behaviors and attitudes on your part and that of your spouse. For example: "Perform a new kind act toward

him/her"; "Give one compliment each day"; "Mentally list my spouse's positive points."

| MY BEHAVIORS<br>AND ATTITUDES | MY SPOUSE'S BEHAVIORS<br>AND ATTITUDES |
|---|---|
| (1) _____ | (1) _____ |
| (2) _____ | (2) _____ |
| (3) _____ | (3) _____ |
| (4) _____ | (4) _____ |
| (5) _____ | (5) _____ |

## Notes

1. John Lavender, *Your Marriage Needs Three Love Affairs* (Denver, CO: Accent Books, 1978).
2. David and Vera Mace, *We Can Have Better Marriages if We Really Want Them* (Nashville: Abingdon Press, 1974), p. 98.
3. David Augsburger, *Cherishable Love and Marriage* (Scottsdale, PA: Herald Press, 1971), p. 97.
4. Harry Hollis, Jr., *Thank God for Sex* (Nashville: Broadman Press, 1975), pp. 11,12. Copyright 1975, used by permission.
5. Lavender, p. 35, 36.
6. John F. Cuber and Peggy B. Haroff, "The more total view: relationships among men and women of the upper middle class," *Marriage and Family Living* (1963), vol. 25, pp. 140–145.
7. Mace, p. 103.
8. Mace, p. 85.

## CHAPTER TWO

# EXCUSES FOR MARITAL DIFFICULTIES

In the first chapter we talked about various styles of marriage. You may have experienced one or more of these styles yourself, or you may have noticed couples in your neighborhood or church whose marriages exhibit the characteristics of these styles. The style of marriage depends on the makeup of the spouses.

In this chapter we will consider the specific behaviors of the five styles of marriage, some of which destroy marriages and thus should be eliminated. As we discuss several types of behavior and the individuals who exhibit them, you will have an opportunity to decide which style of marriage each one would best fit.

**The placater is a martyr.** Always trying to do what he thinks his partner wants is the name of his game. He does not consider his own needs or desires because he fears rejection or disapproval. The placater's way of relating to others is very dishonest because he denies his own feelings and wishes, even though on many occasions he may be right and his partner wrong. He doesn't express (openly, that is) anger, dislike, or disapproval. He doesn't make waves! Because of this type of behavior, trust is absent from the relationship, and he has built for himself an excellent case of isolation, resentment and, very possibly, some physical ills. This behavior does not reflect Christian teachings. The marriage might even improve if the boat were rocked a bit.

*Which style of marriage do you think this person reflects?* Vital, total, passive-congenial, conflict-habituated, or devitalized? (Circle one.)

**The empty lover doesn't like feelings or emotions.** He neither expresses nor really likes to hear feelings, even the positive kind. He avoids expressing them and even makes excuses to leave or changes the subject when his spouse begins to open up. In many cases this response is motivated by fear—fear of being hurt if he were to open up and become vulnerable. This individual who avoids feelings so much is actually controlled by his feelings. In most cases the husband is the empty lover.

All of us have feelings, but the empty lover uses tremendous emotional energy keeping them buried and warding off their onslaught from others. Feelings and emotions, however, when buried are not buried dead. They are buried alive, and at some later time they will be resurrected to haunt us if we refuse to face them and use them in our marriage. The "masculine" John-Wayne-image is working overtime here. The strong, unfeeling, unemotional person may be all right for the westerns, but in the realities of marriage it won't work. God created each person with the same emotions and the same capacity for emotional response. But because of our emotions and experiences we have learned to express or deny our emotions to various degrees. Not to respond is a denial of a gift of God!

*Which style of marriage do you think this person reflects?* Vital, total, passive-congenial, conflict-habituated, or devitalized?

**The smotherers or the 24-hour twosome.** The smotherer is afraid that someday his spouse will discover someone else who is more exciting and then will leave him. So the smotherer tries to tie the other down by "doing everything together."

24

This tactic can be accomplished in two ways: by actually accompanying the partner in all of his activities or by putting roadblocks in his way so he will have a difficult time doing anything alone. Discouraging the other from starting a new venture or overemphasizing the drawbacks or negative points is a dandy way to keep one's spouse under thumb and in one's presence. But this enforced closeness usually puts a greater distance between the two. It shows a lack of trust. Have you ever trusted anyone? Do you trust God? Can you trust yourself?

*Which style of marriage do you think this person reflects?* Vital, total, passive-congenial, conflict-habituated, or devitalized?

**The drill sergeant.** A person who fears criticism may seem like a drill sergeant. Because he fears criticism he becomes hard on himself and his partner. He gives orders to himself and his spouse so that everything in their marriage is "perfect." The house, the way he and his partner dress, the way they perform sexually, the places they select to attend, and the way they throw a party must all be perfect.

The drill sergeant is a doer and has fallen trap to a malady known as the "must syndrome." "I don't have time to talk to you right now, dear, because I must clean. . ."; "We must invite my boss and his wife to the football game because. . ."; "We must attend that church function or. . . ." Musts soon take the fun and joy out of the relationship. If your partner wanted a drill sergeant he/she could have joined the army!

If you are bound by a list of musts, you probably have some preconceived ideas of what your spouse, you, and your relationship should be. Can you distinguish between what "I want" and "I must"? Must is another word for should, and many of our shoulds are very unnecessary.

## WHAT DO YOU THINK?

Do the following learning exercise and you may be surprised by your answers and the results of changing your present pattern.

1. List six personal musts or shoulds, such as "I must have a clean and neat house at all times no matter what!"

2. In response to each "must" above, list what you receive from this must, such as "I feel better about myself" or "I avoid criticism from my mother-in-law (friends, spouse)." Ask yourself what would happen if you didn't fulfill this "must" for a week.

3. What do you really want to do? What could you do with some of the time you take in fulfilling this must?

---

*Which style of marriage do you think the drill sergeant reflects?* Vital, total, passive-congenial, conflict-habituated, or devitalized?

**The tabulator fears being exploited by the other.** He constantly calls attention to himself and builds himself up while downgrading what his partner does. He keeps close records of who does what, and he wants to make sure that each person does his duty! "Me first" is part of his battle cry. This behavior does not reflect Christian compassion or concern for others.

*Which style of marriage do you think this person reflects?* Vital, total, passive-congenial, conflict-habituated, or devitalized?

**The dependent child.** When individuals marry and leave

26

home, they leave physically but the emotional ties are yet to be broken. For some people the emotional separation is too much, or they may be afraid of the separation. The separation may interfere with other relationships. Seeing or calling one's parents too often, constantly asking their advice for decisions, or spending every vacation visiting home may be signs of this problem. Remember—visiting relatives is really just that; it is not a vacation in the true sense of the word!

The book of Genesis states that when one marries he is to leave his mother and father. The words literally mean *abandon, forsake,* or *sever.* This separation is meant in a positive way, but nevertheless there is to be a break.

*Which style of marriage do you think this person reflects?* Vital, total, passive-congenial, conflict-habituated, or devitalized?

**Yet another person is what we call the penny pincher.** Stinginess with money is really just a symptom of some other fear, but it is manifested in a manner that makes the relationship uncomfortable because of checking the money constantly. The tensions to which financial concern leads put pressure upon both individuals. Soon the joy of marriage is lost because of the stress of surviving financially or stashing away as much as possible.

*Which style of marriage do you think this person reflects?* Vital, total, passive-congenial, conflict-habituated, or devitalized?

## WHAT DO YOU THINK?

Let's take a look at your own marriage once again. You may not see yourself or your spouse fitting exactly into any one of these categories, but you may see some tendencies in their direction. Or you may find that one or more fit you like a glove.

1. Which, if any, of the above descriptions seem to fit you as a person?

2. Would your spouse see any of these characteristics in you at this time in your life? Which one(s)?

3. Do you see any of these characteristics in your spouse? Which one(s)?

4. What specifically could a person do to change any of these behavior patterns?

5. What could you do to change if your spouse resists change or will not cooperate?

---

Many marriages begin with a fine foundation, including an extensive courtship period, parental approval, completion of each person's education, premarital preparation through counseling, and even extensive effort during the first few years of marriage to build and develop a quality relationship. But then some time later the marriage falls into trouble. How do marriages become troubled? What does it take for a "vital" marriage to get into trouble?

If a marriage does become troubled, it is important to ask and answer three questions: How did the marriage arrive at this state? How did I contribute to the trouble? What changes can I make at this time to help rebuild my marriage?

You will notice that in these questions there is no mention of what the spouse might be doing wrong. I left out the spouse's behavior purposely, for in most troubled marriages most of the energy and time are used in putting the blame on one's mate for the difficulty. And blaming is futile! One of the greatest detriments to a marital relationship and one that brings on a troubled marriage is blaming one's spouse and making excuses.

When you blame your spouse for the troubled marriage, your mate feels justified in doing the same to you. And if both of you blame and gripe about each other, your energy is exerted, but you're not in gear. No forward progress is made, and often you slide backward. And if you spend your time and energy focusing on the faults and defects in your partner, there is little time and energy left to focus upon your contributions and determine what can be done to help the marriage.

When you find fault you actually show that you oppose your spouse. He/she may make some suggestions or attempts to improve your marriage, but because they are not up to your standard or to your liking, you probably will resist his/her attempts to change! Blaming, finding fault, and using excuses only means that you are investing your energy in defeat!

Blaming means that in a sense you have become a prosecuting attorney seeking to establish the guilt of your partner. But who is the jury and the judge? Will you really convince your spouse? Aren't you both the jury and the judge? Is your spouse innocent until proven guilty, or have you reversed the process?

The Word of God has an answer to blaming and faultfinding: "Stop turning critical eyes on one another. If we must be critical, let us be critical of our own conduct and see that we do nothing to make a brother stumble or fall" (Rom. 14:13, *Phillips*). The Scriptures also tell us to "encourage one another" (see 1 Thess. 5:14).

Sven Wahlroos discusses faultfinding at length in his book *Family Communication:*

"Criticism must be discriminate and take into account the fact that no human being is perfect and that there are many matters which are so unimportant that they should be ignored. . . . When criticism becomes indiscriminate it is called faultfinding and it leads to most destructive consequences. . . .

"1. [These] are the factors which make faultfinding so destructive . . . because of its very definition. It is defined here in terms of communications as a way of saying: 'I do not accept you as a human being because I will not recognize in practice and in daily living that human beings are imperfect.' In other words, faultfinding expresses a lack of acceptance of people and a distorted view of reality.

"2. Because of the basic lack of acceptance involved, faultfinding ruins human relationships, makes people feel hostile toward each other, sours the daily atmosphere of the home and makes it a place of misery rather than of happiness and satisfaction.

"3. Faultfinding is destructive not only to the 'victims' (many of whom are not as innocent as it may appear), but to the faultfinder himself or herself, as well. That is because faultfinding makes the other person either turn you off completely, counterattack or store up resentment against you. . . .

"4. It follows that faultfinding is an ineffective method for changing the behavior of others. It may produce initial results, but if it is kept up it will lead to the other person not really hearing what you are saying; he may hear it in a mechanical sense but it will soon 'go out through the other ear.' Rest assured, however, that the lack of acceptance involved is received and understood.

"5. Thus, faultfinding can be dangerous because when the time comes that you have a truly necessary and important criticism to make, you are powerless then, having diluted the effectiveness of your arguments in advance so that they no longer mean anything to the person being criticized. The danger is especially apparent in the case of children who—through faultfinding—have been taught to think: 'Never mind, it's just that cranky old parent-faultfinder putting on his broken record again.'

"6. Faultfinding teaches unreasonableness and intolerance. Since it induces distaste, it may lead the other party (spouse, child, employee, etc.) to become unreasonable in the other extreme by becoming especially careless and making an excessive number of mistakes, thus setting up a neurotic interaction. . . .

"7. Faultfinding is a consequence of reliance on certain destructive defense mechanisms. The typical faultfinder either projects his own shortcomings onto another person or displaces his anger toward one person (e.g., boss) onto another (e.g., wife). Most often, faultfinding is an unconscious way of trying to hide one's own weaknesses by projecting them onto someone else."[1]

One of the tendencies of human nature is to project blame onto others for difficulties, problems, or circumstances. When people have difficulty in marriage they seem to resort to two procedures: (1) they defend themselves; and (2) they try to discover why the other person does what he/she does. They think they'll be happy when they know *why* the other person acts as he/she does. However, knowing why a person does something doesn't necessarily solve the problem.

Finding out why is not always important, nor is it always possible. What is important is spending time determining what is going on in a relationship and making plans for solving the difficulties or making the changes that are necessary. Reasons may be important at times, but too often they are used as excuses!

Let's look at some typical excuses that people use when they consider why their marriage isn't what they want it to be.[2]

*Some people blame their health:*
*I've had this cold for three months now.*
*I have migraine headaches and. . .*
*I'm just tired all the time.*
*My metabolism is just different than yours.*

31

*Some people blame their feelings:*
   *My nerves are so shaky, and you don't help them at all.*
   *I've been depressed.*
   *The kids make me so upset.*

*Some people blame their nature:*
   *I'm just this way, that's all. I always have been.*
   *I can't change.*
   *I'm a phlegmatic—you know what they're like.*

*Some people blame others:*
   *Her mother is always. . .*
   *His friends are really. . .*
   *It's the darn kids. They just never go to sleep at the right time.*
   *My boss just gets to me. And then. . .*

*Some people blame the past:*
   *She has always been that way.*
   *Nobody has ever liked me and they never will.*
   *My other marriage was lousy too.*
   *My mother always used to put me down.*

*Some people blame their partners:*
   *He makes me so upset I could scream.*
   *If only she'd shut up and listen to me.*
   *He's an animal. All he thinks about is food, TV, and sex, and not in that order either!*
   *If she'd ever clean the house I'd faint.*

*Some people blame "Why":*
   *Why don't we communicate?*
   *If only I could understand why he does. . .*
   *But why can't he stay home on Saturday nights?*

Consider these verses from *The Living Bible:*
"If you refuse criticism you will end in poverty and disgrace; if you accept criticism you are on the road to fame" (Prov. 13:18).

"Timely advice is as lovely as golden apples in a silver basket" (Prov. 25:11).

"A man who refuses to admit his mistakes can never be successful. But if he confesses and forsakes them, he gets another chance" (Prov. 28:13).

"In the end, people appreciate frankness more than flattery" (Prov. 28:23).

And from *The Amplified Bible:*

"He who heeds instruction and correction is [not only himself] in the way of life, but is a way of life for others. And he who neglects or refuses reproof [not only himself] goes astray, but causes to err and is a path toward ruin for others" (Prov. 10:17).

"A soft answer turns away wrath; but grievous words stir up anger" (Prov. 15:1).

"He who refuses and ignores instruction and correction despises himself, but he who heeds reproof gets understanding" (Prov. 15:32).

"A reproof enters deeper into one of understanding than a hundred lashes into a [self-confident] fool" (Prov. 17:10).

"Good sense makes a man restrain his anger, and it is his glory to overlook a transgression or an offense" (Prov. 19:11).

"Open rebuke is better than love that is hidden" (Prov. 27:5).

These verses, also from *The Amplified Bible,* apply to those who make excuses. There is help for us in responding to a person who relies upon excuses:

"Rather, let our lives lovingly express truth in all things— speaking truly, dealing truly, living truly. Enfolded in love, let us grow up in every way and in all things into Him, Who is the Head, [even] Christ, the Messiah, the Anointed One. . . . Therefore, rejecting all falsity and done now with it, let every one express the truth with his neighbor, for we are all parts of one body and members one of another" (Eph. 4:15, 25).

"There are those who speak rashly like the piercing of a

sword, but the tongue of the wise brings healing" (Prov. 12:18).

"A man has joy in making an apt answer, and a word spoken at the right moment, how good it is!" (Prov. 15:23).

"He who answers a matter before he hears the facts, it is folly and shame to him" (Prov. 18:13).

A person who makes excuses may feel threatened or insecure. He may have a poor self-image. If he admits his mistakes, he reinforces his poor self-image. He may be fearful that his admission may be used against him time and time again and that he'll never hear the last of it.

We can help such a person by not accusing or attacking him when we ask a question. When a person admits a mistake or doing something wrong, we can thank the person and then ask if there is anything that we can do to help the situation. The less pressure we put upon the person, the better chance there is for a positive response.

When we can stop thinking about what we can't do in our marriage and why we can't do it, then we can put forth our effort on building the marriage. Excuses accomplish nothing. Excuses do not solve problems; they only create more or postpone the problems. What would happen if we would begin to admit our mistakes? Perhaps others would learn to take pressure off us. If we have children who make excuses and defend themselves, could it be that they learned this pattern of behavior from us? Could they be insecure?

**WHAT DO YOU THINK?**

The Word of God says, "Stop turning critical eyes on one another. If we must be critical, let us be critical of our own conduct and see that we do nothing to make a brother stumble and fall" (Rom. 14:13, *Phillips*). Paul tells us to encourage one another (see 1 Thess. 5:14). Invest your energy in looking at your own contributions to the marriage and develop your own potential and capabilities. In place of excuses take some positive action.

## WHAT'S YOUR PLAN?

Let's look now at the blaming and excuses that may be present in your own marriage.

1. List any blames that you have projected toward your spouse in the last three months.

2. Have any changes occurred because of blaming? If so, indicate what they are.

3. Is your spouse aware of the blaming? If so, how has he/she responded?

4. How do you feel about blaming?

5. Write out one problem for which you blame your partner. Then rewrite it in the form of a constructive, positive suggestion that would be acceptable to him/her.

6. List any excuses you may have made in the past six months as to why your marriage isn't better than it is.

7. What could you do to replace the excuses that you may have made?

8. Ask your spouse to share with you what he/she sees operating in your life. Ask him/her to suggest what you could replace them with. Ask how he/she feels about the musts you have been focusing on.

## Notes

1. Sven Wahlroos, *Family Communication* (New York: Macmillan Co., 1974), pp. 20, 21. Copyright 1974, used by permission.
2. Adapted from Edward Ford, *Why Marriage: A Reality Therapist Looks at Married Life* (Niles, IL: Argus Communication, 1974), p. 19.

## CHAPTER THREE

# THE MOST IMPORTANT ELEMENTS OF MARRIAGE

Any individual or couple can either divert a troubled marriage from the direction it is heading or improve a good marriage. Now that the painful process of soul searching has been completed, the remainder of this book focuses upon improving your marriage.

The first step toward marital enrichment is to be aware of the stages of marriage and what to expect during each of them. Knowing what others have experienced helps make you aware of potential pitfalls in marriage and enables you to handle these unexpected events when and if they do occur.

Many books and other resources are available that describe the marital stages for you. Just as a child progresses through various developmental stages, so does a marriage. Sociological studies have determined common problems in these various stages. Being aware of the potential problems as these stages occur can help a couple plan in advance and perhaps even curtail some of the problems.

All marriages have ups and downs. Some can be avoided, others cannot. No matter how deep your love for each other, certain phases of marriage tend to create difficulties for a couple.

Let's assume that you were married in your early twenties, which is the typical marrying age for couples in our nation. Using this information as a basis, here are some suggested stages. As you read about them, see if you can identify with the various stages.

Before you read the descriptions of these stages, let's see what you believe about them already. Listed below are common problems people encounter at various stages in their marriage relationship. Opposite each potential marital conflict, indicate at which stage you think a couple or individual would most likely encounter the conflict:

Ages 22–28; Ages 29–32; Ages 33–39; Ages 40–43; Ages 44–53; Ages 54–65

_____in-law relationships

_____mother feels "trapped" by growing family

_____loneliness

_____financial problems

_____conflict of outside interest

_____demands of a profession or vocation

_____adjusting to "empty nest"

_____bail-out of family responsibilities

_____increasing closeness to each other

_____decline in marital satisfaction

_____questioning of old standard values

_____competition of carry-over friendships

_____vulnerability to an affair

*Ages 22–28.* Between ages 22 and 28, youthful vigor and enthusiasm give stability to handle disappointment. Since there is little marital history, there is little from the past to influence the couple or to focus upon. Studies indicate that in time the honeymoon glow disappears and some of the happiness disappears.

When the first child arrives, marital satisfaction tends to decline. The marital conflicts that are most likely to occur at this time are in-law relationships, finances, the stress of caring for young children, and outside friendships that carry over from single life. Couples who are most likely to be affected are those who are still emotionally tied to their parents and have

38

not fully developed their emotional ties in their marriage.

*Ages 29–32* can be a difficult time for both individuals. Often the wife, as she cares for a growing family, feels "trapped." The husband feels the pressure of demands at home and in progressing in his profession or vocation. This pressure on both fronts leaves both husband and wife vulnerable to an affair. This is a time when each may be prone to blame the other for their troubles and stresses. Children add to the tension, but childless couples are not immune to these stresses.

*Ages 33–39* can be a more settled time as children are growing and the couple is working toward financial stability. If the marriage is a good one, the couple has learned many methods by which to handle the day-to-day difficulties that arise. This is a time when conflict over control of family decisions can emerge, which may reflect a difference in values and goals. Spouses might feel single even though married, as emotional divorce from each other is common during this stage. An outside activity or interest may drain the intense emotional investment that would otherwise be directed toward the partner.

*Ages 40–43.* Most couples this age are parents of teenagers. This is a time of stress because many teenagers flaunt their budding independence. Many wives are working by now, and many men are realizing that they have reached the limit of their potential on the job. They must both face getting older, but some, in their mad dash to make up for what they have lost in previous years, bail out of their family responsibilities. If the couple has come to this stage with a poor marital relationship, it may explode into the open at this time. Often old standard values are being questioned.

*Ages 44–53.* If the previous stages have been weathered fairly peaceably and the couple has worked upon building their marriage, this stage may be a satisfying one. If the last child has left home, the wife may have reached a depth of dissatisfaction as she adapts to this. But many couples, after adjusting to the empty nest, find this a very satisfying time in their marital experience. In some ways the children represented a bit of a barrier, and with the barrier gone the couple can move closer together.

A new concern at this stage may be the aging of one's parents. Or if children kept the couple together, the pain of a lack of good relationships between each other may be keenly felt at this time. A wife who plunged her life into the needs of her children and never sought to develop her own life will feel lonely at this time. Menopause and the mid-life crisis have their effect on the couple too.

*Ages 54–65* is a time when a couple can reach a high point of satisfaction in their relationship. Companionship can increase, but conflicts may become intense if one partner seeks a deeper relationship and the other continues his life-long pattern of withdrawal.

Later in this chapter several principles will be mentioned which will give couples stability in each of these stages if they spend time implementing them on an ongoing basis.

## WHAT DO YOU THINK?

Let's assume that you are a professional marriage counselor and you have been asked to give a presentation of the 10 most important elements of a marriage relationship. What would you say, and in what order would you present the elements to indicate their importance? Take time now and prepare your presentation. List the 10 items in order of importance.

1.                                    6.

2.                                    7.

3.                                    8.

4.                                    9.

5.                                    10.

Let's compare your list with that of a leading psychologist, Sol Gordon. As director of the Institute for Family Research and Education at Syracuse University, Dr. Gordon has been involved in helping hundreds of married couples. These elements are not listed in order of importance. After you read this list and compare it with your own, you will be asked to put the elements of Dr. Gordon's list in order of importance as you see them, and then you can compare.

1. *Laughter.* Learning how to laugh and developing a sense of humor can give balance to daily life. Look for the humor in a situation instead of letting it tear you apart.

2. *Friendships.* As a couple you have some friends whom you enjoy together, but you also have some that you enjoy by yourself. This is all right and even necessary. Your spouse will be able to meet some of your needs, but there are others who have similar interests and abilities in your hobby or sporting activity, and time spent with them in this pursuit is healthy.

3. *Involvement.* As a couple you have a sense of purpose about something outside your marriage and home. As you work on a meaningful project or endeavor together you have a shared sense of involvement. Some couples teach a Sunday School class together or serve on a committee together. In my own situation I do a great deal of teaching at a college, in churches, and in seminars across the country. I am up in front speaking and teaching. Joyce, my wife, is never in front, but she is directly involved in my ministry. She prepares all of my hundreds of overhead transparencies. She knows the content of my presentations and is just as involved as if she were the one teaching.

4. *Sex.* Sexual fulfillment is an expression of shared intimacy. In order to be fulfilling sex needs loving with it. Too many couples become blasé in their sexual relationship so that it becomes humdrum. I have encouraged many couples to read *Solomon on Sex* by Joseph Dillow (published by Thomas Nelson) for some practical suggestions on continuing

the romantic side of sexuality. Sex is a part of marriage, but for some couples it is quite overrated as the main benefit of marriage.

5. *Sharing*. This means sharing thoughts, information, jobs, projects, etc. It involves the unpleasant as well as the pleasant. As I am writing this book, we are in the process of helping a new shelty puppy adjust to our household. She is our second shelty, and she is a potential bride for our male. Her name is Amber, but "Puddles" would be more fitting right now! Whenever Joyce or I walk through the kitchen area (and never in bare feet!), we look for the signs that Amber is awake and roaming about. When a puddle is sighted, whoever sees it cleans it up and scrubs that section of the floor. We don't call the other person to do it.

The artificiality of the male and female role structure in the home is gradually changing, and the change allows for a greater possibility of sharing based upon ability, giftedness, and cooperation rather than upon a rigid structure.

6. *Integrity*. Being a person who is dependable and trustworthy and not compromising one's beliefs and standards is a reflection of integrity.

7. *Talk*. Conversation that is interesting and informative and contains information and emotions is an asset to a marriage. Open and honest communication that is free from fear of revealing one's own feelings of interfering in the feelings of others is important.

8. *Love* involves caring, intimacy, trust, and commitment. Consistent large and small sensitive behaviors convey love just as the words do. Involved in love is liking the other person and desiring to be with him/her.

9. *Adaptability* involves acceptance of the other person's uniqueness. Adaptability is accepting the other person as he is, without endeavoring to make him a Xerox copy of oneself. It means allowing the other person to do and be other than exactly what you expect.

10. *Tolerance*. Another word for this trait is acceptance. Accepting the other's quirks, occasional forgetfulness, and disagreeable moods means allowing your partner to be human just as you are. When you need to express your displeasure or concern, do it in such a way that it helps the relationship rather than hinders it.[1]

## WHAT DO YOU THINK?

In the first column, list Dr. Gordon's elements of marriage in the order of importance as you see them. In the second column indicate how you think your spouse would structure the list.

| How I Rank Dr. Gordon's Marriage Elements | How I Think My Spouse Would Rank These Elements |
|---|---|
| 1. | 1. |
| 2. | 2. |
| 3. | 3. |
| 4. | 4. |
| 5. | 5. |
| 6. | 6. |
| 7. | 7. |
| 8. | 8. |
| 9. | 9. |
| 10. | 10. |

Ask your spouse to list the 10 in order of importance. When you finish these three lists, turn to the end of this chapter to see how Dr. Gordon ranks the 10 elements of marriage. Discuss with your spouse how each of you ranked your lists, then discuss the difference between your lists and Dr. Gordon's list. Now compare your original list in the previous WHAT DO YOU THINK? section with your spouse's original list. Did you have

If I were to read both of your lists I probably would agree with many you included just as I agree with many of Dr. Gordon's elements of marriage. However, I would like to give you eight key elements I feel are crucial to a marriage. Many of these areas incorporate items on Dr. Gordon's list and many may incorporate items on your list. But I believe the following eight areas are basic to a successful marriage. They are the eight pillars of marriage, and discussion of these make up the remainder of this book.

1. *Goals.* Individual goals and marital goals lend direction to a marriage relationship. Far too many couples drift through their marriage with little direction. In fact, in surveying thousands of couples in the past few years, I have found only approximately four percent discussed, developed and implemented goals for their marriage. "Live life, then, with a due sense of responsibility, not as men [and women] who do not know the meaning and purpose of life but as those who do" (Eph. 5:15,16, *Phillips*).

2. *Expectations for marriage.* Each individual enters marriage with both an overt and a hidden set of expectations for the marriage and the partner's behavior and performance. As the marriage proceeds, some are brought to the surface and some linger beneath. When these expectations are all brought into the open, evaluated, challenged and discussed, greater harmony comes to the marriage. "And he shall be like a tree firmly planted [and tended] by the streams of water, ready to bring forth his fruit in its season; his leaf also shall not fade or wither, and everything he does shall prosper [and come to maturity]" (Ps. 1:3, *AMP*).

3. *Determining needs.* Most couples, whether they realize it or not, marry for need satisfaction. Undefined and unclear needs, however, create frustration for both husband and wife.

Clarifying these needs will enhance all phases of the marriage. Along with clarifying needs, specific steps of implementing positive behaviors in the marriage need to be explored. "Let each of you esteem and look upon and be concerned for not [merely] his own interests, but also each for the interests of others" (Phil. 2:4, *AMP*).

4. *Handling change and crisis in marriage* is an area in which most couples are poorly prepared. Too many couples are unaware that each partner will make many personal changes during the course of their marriage, and each change can affect the stability and functioning of the marriage. Most couples anticipate a crisis-free marriage, but loss of a home, job, child, position in the community, etc., can occur. Are we prepared to handle these crises? Do we know what to do and what resources we can draw upon? James 1:2,3 (*AMP*) tells us to "Consider it wholly joyful, my brethren, whenever you are enveloped in or encounter trials of any sort, or fall into various temptations. Be assured and understand that the trial and proving of your faith bring out endurance and steadfastness and patience."

5. *Decision-making.* Who exerts the greatest amount of power in the marriage, and is this arrangement the best? Who makes the decisions? What contribution does each make? What if one is a fast thinker and the other a slow responder? How does the contribution of each affect the decision-making process? Who is best qualified to decide? What kind of a model for decision-making is being presented to the children? "Be subject to one another out of reverence for Christ, the Messiah, the Anointed One" (Eph. 5:21, *AMP*).

6. *Conflict resolution.* Naturally this involves communication. If couples could determine the cause of the conflicts and develop a logical procedure for resolving the conflict, greater marital stability would come earlier in the marriage. "Then let us no more criticize and blame and pass judgment on one another, but rather decide and endeavor never to put a

stumbling block or an obstacle or a hindrance in the way of a brother" (Rom. 14:13, *AMP*).

7. *Prayer.* Why are many Christian couples embarrassed about praying together? The individual and corporate prayer life of couples can provide a stability that is refreshing, enjoyable, and helpful to the ongoing health of the marriage. "Again I tell you, if two of you on earth agree (harmonize together, together make a symphony) about—anything and everything—whatever they shall ask, it will come to pass and be done for them by My Father in heaven. For wherever two or three are gathered (drawn together as My followers) in (into) My name, there I AM in the midst of them" (Matt. 18:19, 20, *AMP*).

8. *Forgiveness.* Couples allow past behaviors to influence and hinder their relationship. True forgiveness is perhaps risky but so refreshing and life-giving. "And become useful and helpful and kind to one another, tenderhearted (compassionate, understanding, lovinghearted), forgiving one another [readily and freely], as God in Christ forgave you" (Eph. 4:32, *AMP*).

No matter which of these elements you settle upon, each becomes a pillar of marriage. Marriage can be likened to a house supported and stabilized by these pillars.

DIAGRAM 7

**THE PILLARS OF MARRIAGE**

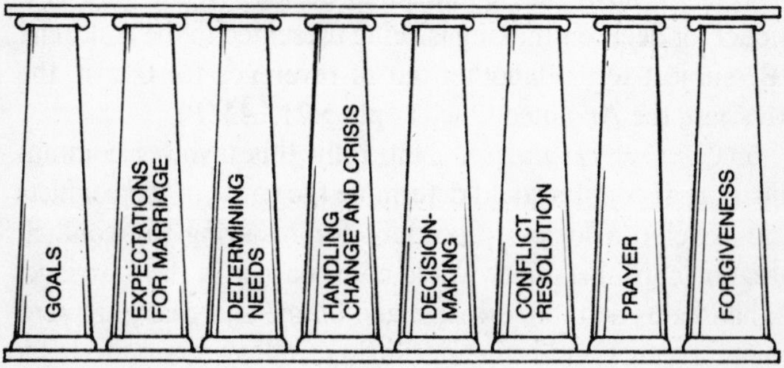

GOALS — EXPECTATIONS FOR MARRIAGE — DETERMINING NEEDS — HANDLING CHANGE AND CRISIS — DECISION-MAKING — CONFLICT RESOLUTION — PRAYER — FORGIVENESS

If one of the pillars crumbles or wears away because the caretaker ignores the condition of the house (in this case, marriage), the house must stand upon the remaining pillars. If another pillar is taken away, the house becomes even weaker. The remaining pillars will finally erode and the house will crumble. So it is with marriage. God has created us male and female. He has given us marriage. He has a plan for our marriage, but the choice of what we do with our marriage is ours.

## WHAT'S YOUR PLAN?

1. What pillars do you now have for your marriage?

2. Which pillars would you like to strengthen, which would you like to replace, and which do you feel should be established?

3. Indicate three specific steps you could take to strengthen an existing pillar or construct a new one.

4. How do you think your spouse would answer these first three questions?

5. Go back through the chapter again. Using your own list, Dr. Gordon's list, and my suggestions, construct your own list of 12 pillars of marriage you think are most essential. Then list them in order of importance. Ask your spouse to do the same, and then discuss them together and determine what you can do to strengthen each of them.

(1)                              (7)

(2)                              (8)

(3)                              (9)

(4)                              (10)

(5)                              (11)

(6)                              (12)

Note: Here is Dr. Gordon's list in order of importance from his point of view:

1. Love                          6. Integrity
2. Laughter                      7. Tolerance
3. Talk                          8. Adaptability
4. Involvement                   9. Sex
5. Friendships                   10. Sharing

**Note**

1. Sol Gordon, "10 Most Important Things in Marriage," *Good Housekeeping*, April 1978, pp. 58–60.

## CHAPTER FOUR

# EXPECTATIONS AND GOALS IN MARRIAGE

The setting and attainment of goals in marriage is one of the most neglected essentials for marital growth. The manner in which a marriage develops and what it reflects is a couple's choice. If a couple has set well-defined marital goals and has developed strategies and plans to attain the goals, their relationship will continually grow.

Before you set goals for your marriage, you need to think about your expectations for marriage. We all enter marriage assuming that certain events will transpire and that our relationships will develop in a certain way. These expectations often remain unspoken, even after we are married. Because our spouse is unaware of them, often they are not fulfilled.

What expectations do you have for your marriage, and what expectations does your spouse have? Are they realistic? Can they really be met? Bringing expectations into the open and examining them is necessary.

In premarital counseling I ask the couples as individuals to list 25 expectations they have for their future spouses to fulfill after they are married. Then I ask them to write a short paragraph describing the effect each expectation will have on their marriage if it is not met. Each person reads his/her future spouse's list of expectations and decides which expectations are reasonable and attainable and which are not.

You may not have had an opportunity to share your expectations in premarital counseling. If not, now is a good time to look at some of your expectations. Being aware of your expectations is the first step in setting goals.

1. Indicate five expectations you had for your partner when you first married.

2. What are five expectations you have at the present time?

3. What are your spouse's expectations for you, and how do you know?

4. Indicate which of the expectations listed above are realistic and which are not.

---

A goal is something we would like to achieve or see happen. A goal is a statement involving faith, for it tells of something we hope will happen in the future. "Faith is the substance of things hoped for" (Heb. 11:1, *KJV*). We all have goals, dreams, or objectives, and we proceed through life responding to these goals. How we are living is determined by the goal toward which we are working. Clearly defined goals give clarity to life, whereas muddled, hazy, unclear goals lead to confusion, purposelessness, and depression. "Where there is no vision the people run wild" (Prov. 29:18, *Berkeley*).

Our goals motivate us toward the future. But what are our goals built upon—our needs, our wants, our own dreams, our spouses, our parents?

At this stage of your life you have probably attained numerous goals. Take time now to evaluate what you have accomplished so far in life.

## WHAT DO YOU THINK?

1. List five goals that you have personally achieved in the past 10 years. Also indicate what you did to accomplish these goals.

| GOALS | STEPS I TOOK TO REACH THEM |
|-------|---------------------------|
| (1) | (1) |
| (2) | (2) |
| (3) | (3) |
| (4) | (4) |
| (5) | (5) |

2. What has been accomplished in your marriage during the time you've been married?

3. Are you satisfied with this accomplishment? If so, could you be even more satisfied with the establishment of specific goals? Which one(s)?

4. What specifically are you getting out of marriage that you would not have gotten if you had remained single?

5. How much time do you spend each week enhancing or enriching your marriage?

6. Indicate specifically what you did during the past month to enrich your marriage and how much time you spent for each activity or event.

| WEEK | ACTIVITY | TIME |
|------|----------|------|
| 1st | | |
| 2nd | | |
| 3rd | | |
| 4th | | |

7. What amount of money have you set aside for marital enrichment?

---

The importance of goals has been stressed by psychiatrist Ari Kiev of the Cornell Medical Center: "With goals people can overcome confusion and conflict over incompatible values, contradictory desires and frustrated relationships with friends and relatives, all of which often result from the absence of rational life strategies.

"Observing the lives of people who have mastered adversity, I have repeatedly noted that they have established goals and, irrespective of obstacles, sought with all their effort to achieve them. From the moment they've fixed an objective in their mind and decide to concentrate all their energies on a specific goal, they begin to surmount the most difficult odds."[1]

Goals give you a sense of direction. They are not what *will* be, but what you hope will be attained. Because they are future oriented, they can lift us from some of the difficulties of our present situation. Our focus can be upon positive hopes to come. As Christians we live in the present and future. Scripture admonishes us to have purposes and direction for our lives. "Forgetting the past and looking forward to what lies ahead, I strain to reach the end of the race" (Phil. 3:13,14, *TLB*). "A man's mind plans his way, but the Lord directs his steps" (Prov. 16:9, *RSV*). Once we set goals, our steps can be directed by the Lord.

Goals will help you use your time more effectively, for they help you sort out what is important and what is not. If you know what you intend or need to do, it is much easier to keep from being sidetracked.

I have a list of demands placed upon my time for ministry to others. Some time ago I determined how much time I have available for my speaking ministry each month, what I feel needs to be accomplished during these times of ministry, and how best to accomplish the objectives. It is far easier now to evaluate requests and to say no to those that could detract me from the original, God-directed goal.

As we decide upon goals, we need to realize that a goal is an event in the future that is accomplishable and measurable. If I say that I want to be a good swimmer, I am stating a purpose. If I say that I want to be able to swim six laps in an Olympic-size pool by July 1, I am stating a goal.

Here are the characteristics of well-stated goals.

1. *A goal should be stated in terms of the end result.* Example: Spend two hours per week in direct, face-to-face communication with my wife.

2. *A goal should be achievable in a definite time period.* Example: Spend two hours per week in direct, face-to-face communication with my wife *by the end of February.*

3. *A goal should be definite as to what is expected.* Example: Spend two hours per week in *direct, face-to-face communication* with my wife by the end of February.

4. *A goal should be practical and feasible.* Example: Spend *two hours per week* in direct, face-to-face communication with my wife by the end of February.

5. *A goal should be stated precisely in terms of quan-*

*tities where applicable.* Example: Spend *two hours per week* in direct, face-to-face communication with my wife by the end of February.

6. *A goal should have one important goal or statement* rather than several.

Here is a list of goals written by a young woman in pre-marital counseling. She had been asked to select goals for her marriage. She was also asked to select a goal for her own life that she would like to achieve within three years and a goal for her fiance to achieve within three years.

*By three months:*

☐ 1. Make the first four minutes together each day (morning, evening, etc.) a quality time of building, affirming, and affection.

☐ 2. Pray together daily (intercession, praise—more than just for meals); pray together on our knees in a 10- to 15-minute session once a week.

☐ 3. Study the Bible together once a week in addition to individual quiet times and/or reading Scripture at supper.

*By six months:*

☐ 4. Refine communication patterns so that we go to sleep only after each partner is satisfied that he/she is understood and accepted by the other and that all is forgiven.

☐ 5. Practice hospitality—have children, another couple, or a friend over for a meal twice a month.

☐ 6. Have feedback once a month on how marriage is going. Take 2- to 3-hour blocks and discuss growth and satisfactions as well as dissatisfactions and "unimportant things."

*By one year:*

☐ 7. Improve sexual patterns—creative, satisfying, and exciting to both partners most of the time; understanding partner's moods, etc.

☐ 8. Be able to draw out the best in each of us; seek constructive criticism from each other, and be able to give it.

*Three-year goal for him—self-image*

☐ To see himself as worthy, having much to offer the psychological, evangelical, and his interpersonal worlds (i.e., not get depressed) regardless of accomplishments.

*Three-year goal for me—flexibility*

☐ To be flexible—able to take the other side, back down and admit I'm wrong in an argument; to be tolerant of others' views; to enjoy spontaneous guests for dinner, or being a spontaneous guest for dinner.

## WHAT DO YOU THINK?

Are the six characteristics of well-stated goals evident in this young woman's goals? In the squares before each of her goals, indicate which one(s) of the six characteristics are included. Use numbers 1 through 6.

What can you do now to discover and set your goals? Ed Dayton and Ted Engstrom, in their book *Strategy for Living,* have given seven steps to setting goals. Respond to each of the following steps in the space provided. (You may want to review the difference between a goal and a purpose at this time.)

*Step 1: Understand your purpose.* What is it that you would like to do or for your marriage to become? What is the general direction toward which you would like your marriage to move? Make a statement about that.

*Step 2: Picture the situation.* Imagine the situation of your marriage not as it is now, but as you would like it to be. What does it look like? Who are you with? What are you doing? What are the circumstances? Visualize and use your mental imagery.

*Step 3: State some long-range goals.* What measurable and accomplishable events would have to happen in order for that purpose to be realized?

*Step 4: State your immediate goals.* What are the things that you have to accomplish now if you are going to move toward your ultimate purpose in your marriage?

*Step 5: Act.* Pick out one of the goals for your marriage and start moving toward it. Remember that every long journey begins with the first step!

*Step 6: Act as if...* Act as if you have already reached your goal. If you are going to start working toward that first goal, you are going to have to start acting as if you had really reached it. How would this impact on all the other parts of your life? What would it say about your plans for your church, your family, others? This may help you uncover some other goals that you need to consider.

*Step 7: Keep praying.* If you are going to live life with a purpose, then you need to keep seeking God's leading in all this. Yes, you have been praying through the whole planning process. But pray, as well, before you act. If you are expecting to live a life with God's purpose in mind, you had better be communicating with Him.[2] Read Jeremiah 33:3.

**WHAT DO YOU THINK?**

1. What do you want your marriage to reflect? Now is the time for you as an individual to begin setting some goals for your marital relationship. Using the information stated in this chapter, develop eight goals for your marriage. Here are a few ideas that may help you. I want my marriage to reflect goals in: finances, time spent together, recreation, roles and responsibilities, home life, ministry to other couples, sex life. Our marriage should have goals for: prayer and Bible study together, location and times of vacation, quantity of communication, trust in our relationship,

and resolving conflict. (Please work by yourself. Ask your spouse to do the same in his book or on a piece of paper. Do not discuss or compare your goals at this point.)

(1)

(2)

(3)

(4)

(5)

(6)

(7)

(8)

2. Do all of these goals meet the criteria of the six characteristics for well-stated goals?

_____

Now that you have developed your goals, evaluate them in terms of your priorities. How do you know if these are the best goals for your marriage? What if there are too many goals and you are overwhelmed by them?

**WHAT DO YOU THINK?**

_____

Consider these questions.

1. How urgent are your goals? When must they be accomplished for you and for the health of your marriage? Right away? A year from now?




2. How important are they (circle one)? Very? Quite? Somewhat? So-so?

3. How often must you make an effort toward achieving your goals (circle one)? Daily? Weekly? Occasionally?

4. What will happen to you and your marriage if these goals are not accomplished (circle one)? An explosion? Disaster? Upset? Nothing? If nothing or little at all, what does that tell you about their priority?

5. Are these the best goals, or could there be better ones?

---

The ABC technique of placing goals in order of priority may help you in this task. Assign each goal a value of A, B, or C.

A = "must do" (high value)

B = "should do" (medium value)

C = "can do" (low value)

If you have too many "A" goals, you may want to subdivide them into $A_1$, $A_2$, etc. This process will help you narrow the field.

### WHAT DO YOU THINK?

1. Go back over your list of goals and evaluate each one with an A, B, or C. Place the letter on the left side of the page.

2. When you have completed this task, go back and evaluate your goals as you think your spouse would. Then place the A, B, or C on the right side of the page.

3. Now evaluate your marital goals with the following questions:

a. How does each goal reflect your commitment to or relationship with Jesus Christ?

(1)

(2)

(3)

(4)

(5)

(6)

(7)

(8)

b. How would the attainment of each goal affect your Christian life?

(1)

(2)

(3)

(4)

(5)

(6)

(7)

(8)

c. How would the attainment of each goal present a witness to the presence of Christ in your life?

(1)

(2)

(3)

(4)

(5)

(6)

(7)

(8)


    d. How will the attainment of each goal enrich the personal life of your spouse?

(1)

(2)

(3)

(4)

(5)

(6)

(7)

(8)

---

    Goal-setting and priority-evaluation are not all of the process, however. Developing your plan to attain the goal is the heart of the process. Planning moves you from the present to the future.

    You must be flexible and adaptable, because plans do change. Locking yourself into a dead-end approach would be as detrimental to your marriage as no goal-setting at all. This fact is stated in the book of Proverbs: "It is pleasant to see plans develop. That is why fools refuse to give them up even when they are wrong" (13:19, *TLB*). Planning is a tool, a means to an end. It saves time and energy and decreases frustration.

    One husband described how he and his wife learned to plan their goals: "Before we were married, Evie's and my goals were just to get married. In the beginning years of our marriage, our major goals centered around my finishing seminary and getting into ministry. There were no goals for our life together as a couple except to be happy. Our first real mutual goal was to have a baby. It took us quite some time to realize that goal. Then it wasn't until we were in a seminar—a Christian Marriage Enrichment Seminar—about six years into our marriage that we thought about making mutual goals. This involved deciding upon them together and making them priorities in our lives.

"The experience in the seminar of setting mutual goals and then within the next few months working to reach some of those goals was so beneficial to our marriage that we decided to keep setting and reviewing goals periodically. So we began to set aside a couple of days between two and four times a year to do this. They became what we like to call 'honeymoon weekends.' They may not be on a weekend. We sometimes go away on a Tuesday and Wednesday or Thursday and Friday. The principle is that we get away from our regular routine and demands on our time and we go someplace where we can spend sufficient time together.

"We start on the first afternoon and evening by discussing goals that we previously set and evaluating the progress we've made. We also discuss setbacks and what adjustments we might need to make to reach the goals. We review the goals. About some goals we have made previously, we say, 'Well, that is not realistic,' or 'That is not practical,' or 'That is not so much a priority now as it was when we talked about it last time.'

"Then we spend some time on the second day of our 'honeymoon weekend' talking about goals that involve others. We talk about where we would like to be in five years as a couple and as parents, as ministers, as people in our neighborhood— trying to take into account all aspects of life, including our relationship with God. Then we talk about what we would like to be doing a year from the present time in order to be on our way toward those five-year goals. We discuss intermediate steps that we need to be taking a year from now. Then we talk about what we need to do in the next three months to get started from where we are or to continue from where we are toward the goal where we want to be within a year.

"Some of the goals that we have set were to establish a devotional life together; to establish a family devotional life— later when our kids came along; to involve Evie in further schooling; and to develop my own doctoral program."

## WHAT DO YOU THINK?

Use the following outline to develop your own plans. Select one of the goals that you wrote earlier.

1. Describe your goal in detail using the guidelines suggested.

2. Describe your present situation.

3. What are some of the factors involved in your life or in your marriage that are possibly keeping you from reaching your goal? (We call these "saboteurs.")

4. What helpful or positive factors will assist you in the attainment of your goal?

5. Indicate three specific steps you can take to reach your goal:

62

(1)

(2)

(3)

6. Are these steps practical? Can you think of alternatives?


## WHAT'S YOUR PLAN?

1. Let's go back to the eight goals you wrote earlier. Add four more goals to the list and then share and discuss your list with your spouse. List all 12 goals:

(1)                          (7)
(2)                          (8)
(3)                          (9)
(4)                          (10)
(5)                          (11)
(6)                          (12)

Your spouse's goals:

(1)                          (7)
(2)                          (8)
(3)                          (9)
(4)                          (10)
(5)                          (11)
(6)                          (12)

2. Spend time comparing your lists, and together select 12 that you agree upon. List and evaluate your goals now:

| GOAL | TIME RANGE (SHORT OR LONG) | EXACT TIME |
|------|----------------------------|------------|
| (1)  |                            |            |
| (2)  |                            |            |
| (3)  |                            |            |
| (4)  |                            |            |

**(5)**

**(6)**

**(7)**

**(8)**

**(9)**

**(10)**

**(11)**

**(12)**

3. To the left of each number evaluate your goals in terms of priorities by placing an A, B, or C by each one.

4. Now indicate whether you feel each goal is a short-range goal (1 week, 1 month, 3 months, 6 months, 9 months, 1 year) or a long-range goal (2 or more years).

5. Together develop your detailed plan according to the steps discussed previously. (Use a large piece of paper.) Follow this sequence for each goal:

(1) Goal

(2) Present situation

(3) Factors sabotaging

(4) Helpful or positive factors

(5) Specific steps

6. Indicate your time plan for the next year for continual planning and evaluation of goals.

---

One couple found New Year's Day a good time to set goals and make plans: "New Year's celebration is a special time for my wife and me, as it is a special time to look back and forward. Back—over the past year, enabling us to see how God has blessed us, and to see how our objectives have been met in both our personal and family lives. Forward—in that this is the time set aside for establishing future objectives, reviewing life goals, and evaluating our ability to meet our life purpose.

"For us, our basic purpose lies in giving glory to God, and our family motto is based on Habakkuk 2:14. Therefore, our life goals and personal objectives ultimately are designed to meet that life purpose. For Rita and me, setting a goal is a statement of faith that takes the emphasis off our problems and focuses our lives on future possibilities. The fulfillment of previous objectives is positive reinforcement for persevering into the future.

"One thing we were quick to learn early in our marriage is that if we don't set our own goals, others will set them for us, and their goals may not be ours and may not help us achieve our purpose. In our home it is extremely important to share goals and objectives in order that family members can support one another.

"We're very careful in our choice of life goals as they are the general statement of what we are to *be*. If we are too specific or too restrictive in our choice of life goals, we do not give God's Spirit a chance to work in our lives, or when He does we are frustrated or disappointed with God's will for us. If my whole life focused on a vocation—for example, becoming a physician—what would happen to my life if I failed to meet the requirements for medical school or could not meet the competition? I may see my entire life as a failure and find no further reason to live. But if my life goals are to 'invest my life in others' and I fail to make it into medical school, then there are still many ways open to me to invest my life in others. Even though an objective is not met, my life goals are still intact and I merely have to set new objectives. The battle is lost, but not the war, and I have plenty of reason to go on.

"For Rita and me it is exciting to look back over 12 years of marriage and be able to recount the objectives we have met and to see our life goals continually being met. Each year is special and each succeeding year is more special to us. Our objectives grow in direct proportion to our willingness to step out in faith. God has enriched our lives, and we can list the manifold blessings as they have unfolded before us.

"Our goals do something else for us. As we pray them into our lives, they are constantly before us and regularly reviewed. We find ourselves acting as though those goals were already fulfilled. We focus on the positive aspect of what that goal will do for us. Each objective will help me to meet my life goal, and fulfilled life goals mean I do give glory to God. If we give glory to God, our life has meaning and we find ourselves satisfied and having a real sense of achievement in our lives."

**Notes**

1. Ari Kiev, *A Strategy for Daily Living* (New York: Free Press, 1973), p. 3.
2. Adapted from Edward R. Dayton and Ted W. Engstrom, *Strategy for Living* (Glendale, CA: Regal Books, 1976), pp. 55, 56.

## CHAPTER FIVE

# FULFILLING NEEDS IN MARRIAGE

The amount of satisfaction that you experience in your marriage is directly related to the fulfillment of your needs. One of the reasons why people marry is their hope of satisfying their needs. A need is something we have to have, something that is vital to wholeness in each of us.

How do you meet your needs? By yourself or do you rely solely upon your spouse to meet them? If a couple relies upon each other to meet their needs, the couple is very mutually dependent. The more you *must* have from your spouse, the greater the dependency. Is dependency good or bad? Should we be dependent upon our husband or wife for need satisfaction? Could dependency ever create mutual misery? Does our growth depend upon what our spouse does for us?

**WHAT DO YOU THINK?**

List five needs that you would like your spouse to fulfill:

1.

2.

3.

4.

5.

Realistic need fulfillment is essential for a person's satisfaction and development. Some of our "needs," however, may be "wants." Wants are things that would be nice to have but that we can continue to exist without. It is important to analyze both our needs and our wants to determine which are realistic and which are not.

What type of needs do we have? Are we all alike in our basic needs, and can they all be satisfied in the same manner? There are many different ways to consider needs, and perhaps one of the easiest is to consider a simple structure called the "hierarchy of needs," developed by Abraham Maslow. He suggested that we have five basic needs. The lowest one in the hierarchy must be met before a person is motivated to reach for the next one.

The five needs, starting with the most basic, are:

1. Physical—air, water, food—whatever is necessary to stay alive.

2. Safety—security, freedom from danger, confidence that our physical needs will be met.

3. Love and belonging—being wanted, cared about, listened to, accepted, understood, feeling important, receiving empathy.

4. Self-esteem—attention, respect, significance, value, achievement.

5. Self-actualization—creative potential, being autonomous, ability to give love (*agape*) and to fulfill one's potential or giftedness.

The first four needs are basically taking-in; they are self-centered. Before we can really reach the final need, we must pass through the first four stages. Our physical and personal needs must be met before we can hope to become self-actualized.

John Powell said, "There is one need so fundamental and so essential that if it is met, everything else will almost certainly harmonize in a general sense of well-being. When this need is properly nourished, the whole human organism will be healthy and the person will be happy. This need is a true and deep appreciation of oneself, a genuine and joyful self-acceptance, an authentic self-esteem, which results in an interior sense of celebration: It is good to be me . . . I am very happy to be me."[1]

Some people become stuck at one of the early stages and appear to have an insolvable need for more. They never seem to be satisfied or to get enough, and so they place a high priority upon fulfilling this need. These people may be classified as takers. They cannot give, and in a relationship they constantly drain from the other person.

In seeking a marital partner, the taker may look for one he can become very dependent upon. This dependency may appear to be satisfactory for a time, but what happens if shortly after marriage you discover that your partner is just like you—a taker or a dependent personality? Or if your spouse is one who is generous, sensitive, and giving, he/she could tire of being just a giver and never a recipient.

Some of us enter adulthood with needs that were not adequately met in childhood, such as love, security, and belonging. Often these early unmet needs freeze into rigid behavior patterns and enter our marriage with us. Our adult behavior is then based upon these unmet needs from our childhood. These are called *frozen needs*. They are like recordings that play over and over. And frozen needs cannot be met in the present.

If our unmet need is security or attention, we may at times feel fulfilled, but soon the emptiness returns and we place unrealistic demands upon our partner to fulfill these needs. We tend to see our partner as someone to be used to meet the need.

Occasionally I counsel someone who has an excessive need to be "perfect." The need to be perfect was created in this person by his parents when he was a child. He soon learned that in order to gain acceptance his behavior had to be superior to others. Acceptance from the parents is held out in front of the child like a carrot before a horse—he must always forge ahead and do better. This person learns to belittle his own efforts. He must always strive to do better but does not accept his own efforts. Hugh Missildine described the behavior in this way:

"The perfectionist person has great trouble in finding an acceptable marriage partner, for he wants a 'perfect' mate, not a human one. Thus he tends to reject potential mates, often until he has delayed marriage for years. He has difficulty forming a relationship that would be close enough to lead to marriage. Some such persons give up the attempt to form close human ties and devote themselves to work, not realizing that it lies within their power to alter their attitude toward themselves. This is the situation of some of our successful bachelors and striving career girls.

"The perfectionistic person often looks upon marriage as another achievement. Once married, he does not know how to enjoy it. He generally continues his old perfectionistic attitudes, demanding perfect order. He becomes anxious if the house is not in order at all times, with eggs done to a split-second three minutes, toast to a certain shade of tan, shirts starched a certain way, and perfect children from his perfect wife. His anxiety leads him to demand these things because anything less than what he considers 'perfect' arouses his childhood patterns of self-belittlement. Many a husband silently accepts his perfectionistic wife's demands that he not wear shoes in the living room because she fears marks on her perfect rugs, endures her corrections of his speech, and indeed never feels comfortable himself."[2]

Some people are raised in an atmosphere of neglect, which deprives the man or woman of needed attention. This person may develop in such a way that he lacks the capacity to feel he is important or even to be concerned with others and how they feel. Or he could run from one person to another, hoping that each person will supply the necessary ingredient. He is perpetually dissatisfied with his relationships with others, including his spouse. He longs for a deep, intimate relationship, but the need is so deep that he constantly seeks mothering like a child.

This behavior is unacceptable for an adult, and if his spouse were to get that close, he would be fearful that she would not like him if she really knew him intimately. He has an excessive need for warmth, love, and attention, but he cannot accept it. (This is also true of some women.)

The perfectionist could be a person who was rejected as unaccepted, unwanted, or a nuisance. He has an intense need for two commodities—affection and approval, but he has difficulty believing that the other's love is really sincere! Thus the spouse must continue to give and give and prove his love! The perfectionist sets up "tests" of love which his partner must pass. There is an insatiable demand for love, which can become a pain in time. If the spouse inadvertently or purposely slacks off, the rejection occurs again.

When a need is not met in our marriage, most of our energy goes into having it met. If we have frozen needs, we need to release the painful feelings associated with them. If there is hurt or resentment, inner healing and forgiveness will meet the need.

In addition to frozen needs there are *false needs*. Two examples of this are the false need to be taken care of and the need to take care of another person. Most of these are related hurts or even myths perpetrated upon us in childhood. Some believe that their life will be all right if they find someone to take care of them. When the feelings of inadequacy or helplessness are disposed of and the person discovers he can take care of himself, the need to be looked after or taken care of goes away.

The need to take care of another is also a false need. It too can reflect insecurity; for the person who has to control or take charge of others uses this need to cover inadequacy.

Lawrence Crabb said, "A sign of maturity is the ability to give to others and to meet others' needs. But it appears that in order to do this, we must have the first four levels of needs met. As Christians, you and I have a greater opportunity to have our needs met than others. God has promised to meet all of the needs indicated on Maslow's list. God has met our physical needs. 'Seek ye first the kingdom of God, and his righteousness; and all these things (referring to food, clothing, shelter) shall be added unto you' (Matt. 6:33). God has met our need to know that tomorrow our physical needs will be met. 'Take therefore no (anxious) thought for tomorrow' (Matt. 6:34). 'Be anxious for nothing, but in everything . . . let your requests be made known to God . . . my God shall supply all your needs according to His riches in glory in Christ Jesus' (Phil. 4:6,19). God has met our need for security (love). 'Who shall separate us from the love of Christ? . . . I am persuaded that . . . [nothing] shall be able to separate us from the love of God, which is in Christ Jesus' (Rom. 8:35,38,39). 'God commendeth his love toward us, in that, while we were yet sinners (at our worst, exposed for what we really are, no masks), Christ died for us' (Rom. 5:8). God has met our need for significance (purpose). 'For to me to live is Christ and to die is gain' (Phil. 1:21). 'For we are his workmanship, created in Christ Jesus unto good works, which God hath before ordained that we should walk in them' (Eph. 2:10). '[God] redeemeth thy life from destruction (squandering, wasting)' (Ps. 103:4).

"To the degree that a Christian believes these verses, he is freed from a life of self-centered concern with whether or not his own needs are met, and he is able to move on to real self-actualization, confidently knowing (not necessarily always 'feeling') that his physical needs will be met according to God's purposes and that his personal needs are now and forever perfectly met. To believe this in the face of tremendous pressure to agree with the world's false value system of living for money, pleasure, or fame requires a strong commitment to the authority of Scripture.

"Christians never operate from a deficit but rather from fullness. Our lives should be an expression of that fullness in worship and service. I therefore refer to the motivation of an appropriately self-actualized person as Expression Motivation. Yet most of us feel a deficit and act in ways designed to fill the void. It is one thing to say that we can claim by faith that our needs are already met in God and therefore live in Stage 5 with Expression Motivation. It is quite another thing to disentangle ourselves successfully from the sticky web of deficit motivation."[3]

Another way of considering needs is to look at them from the perspective of the emotional, physical, social-intellectual, and spiritual dimensions. When a couple comes to me for premarital counseling, one of their homework exercises is to identify these needs. Each is asked to evaluate all four areas of need. The area of emotional needs might be the first area that each person would evaluate. Each is asked to list as many emotional needs as possible and then indicate specifically how his future mate can meet each need.

The paper on which each has written his needs is then folded so the specific ways his spouse can meet his needs is covered. They exchange papers, read the specific needs of the other, and then write out what they *think* they can do to meet those needs. Once this is done, they unfold the original paper and compare what they think they can do to meet their partner's needs with what their partner has actually suggested. By doing this, most of the guesswork of need discovery and fulfillment is taken out of marriage, and need satisfaction is greatly enhanced.

Here is what one woman shared in premarital counseling concerning her needs:

## EMOTIONAL

| MY NEEDS | HOW KEN CAN MEET THEM |
|---|---|
| To feel loved, cherished | Call me, prepare me for sex, hold me, kiss me, look at me with glimmer in his eye, take naps so he will feel refreshed to be with me. |
| To feel supported, believed in | Pray for me in front of me and secretly as well. Challenge me, praise me, see my potential in specific situations. |
| To feel comforted when down | Hold me, let me cry on his shoulder, feel my hurt with me, be gentle and sensitive to my moods, let me know he notices them. |
| To feel not alone | Share my daily life's joys and sorrows, enter into the conversation about my day, be interested in daily details that help him understand me. |
| To feel free to be myself, to be genuine | Be himself, be genuine, see through my masks and let me know it. Know that I love him deep down so he can take my present anger. Accept my goofy antics as me but when he doesn't like them, let me know gently what he prefers instead and give me the opportunity to change it. |

## SOCIAL

| MY NEEDS | HOW KEN CAN MEET THEM |
|---|---|
| To get together with other women | Encourage me to get to know friends and neighbors when I feel |

| | timid, and ask me what I learned afterward. |
|---|---|
| To get together as a couple with friends | Be himself, laugh at himself, at me, at us, and share it with others. Be as uninhibited as he dares. |
| To do something spontaneous | Go out to dinner, movies, friend's house, miniature golfing, TV show, something new—surprise me! |
| To get away from the house and schoolwork regularly | Notice when I am useless and suggest a change of pace, just as if he felt cooped up and needed a change. |

Often we attempt to demonstrate our love to our partner by helping and assisting him around the house, but we need to eliminate our preconceived ideas of what would be helpful. We need to discover how he feels about our attempts to help, for these efforts may not be meeting his needs. This is where some of our own behavioral patterns could be changed to enrich the life of our spouse. Ask and listen—even if you think you have a better idea or way. Why not demonstrate your life his way?

## WHAT'S YOUR PLAN?

People are motivated to meet their own needs. If they are hungry, they try to secure food. If they are insecure, they try to find love. Until our needs are met, we operate from a deficit. As we realize how God has met and continues to meet our needs, we become freed from totally concentrating on meeting our needs and can instead seek to meet the needs of our husband or wife.

What are your spouse's needs? Have you ever discussed them? Do you know specifically how you could assist your partner in fulfilling his needs?

1. Without asking your partner, write in the space provided what you think you could do to help fulfill your partner's needs

on the last three levels of Maslow's hierarchy of needs:

| MY PARTNER'S NEEDS | HOW I CAN HELP FULFILL THESE NEEDS |
|---|---|
| Love and belonging | |
| Self-esteem | |
| Self-actualization | |

2. Now share your list with your partner and ask him what he would like you to do to help him fulfill his needs. Write down his responses:

| NEEDS | MY PARTNER'S SUGGESTION |
|---|---|
| Love and belonging | |
| Self-esteem | |
| Self-actualization | |

**Notes**

1. John Powell, *The Secret of Staying in Love* (Niles, IL: Argus Communications, 1974), p. 13.
2. W. Hugh Missildine, *Your Inner Child of the Past* (New York: Simon & Schuster, 1963), p. 91.
3. Lawrence Crabb, *Effective Biblical Counseling* (Grand Rapids: Zondervan, 1977), pp. 83,84.

## CHAPTER SIX

# THREE TYPES OF LOVE

Every person needs to receive love and to give love. These two needs are basic for all people. We demonstrate our inner feelings of love through our behavior. Some of our behaviors are loving and some are not. The Scriptures speak directly about behaviors that we are to "put on" (loving behaviors) and behaviors that we are to "put off" (non-loving behaviors). Look up some of the Scripture references in the list below.

### DIAGRAM 8

"Lay aside every weight, and . . . sin" (Heb. 12:1,2, *KJV*).

| Put Off | Scriptural Insights | Put On |
|---|---|---|
| 1. Lack of love | 1 John 4:7,8,20 <br> John 15:12 | Love |
| 2. Judging | Matthew 7:1,2 <br> John 8:9; 15:22 | Self-examination |
| 3. Bitterness | Hebrews 12:15 <br> Colossians 3:12 | Tenderhearted |
| 4. Unforgiving spirit | Mark 11:25 <br> Matthew 6:14 | Forgiving spirit |
| 5. Pride | Proverbs 16:18 <br> James 4:6 | Humility |
| 6. Boasting (conceit) | 1 Corinthians 4:7 <br> Proverbs 27:2 | Humility |
| 7. Hatred | Matthew 5:21,22 <br> 1 Corinthians 13:3 | Love or kindness |
| 8. Gossip | 1 Timothy 5:13 <br> 1 Peter 2:9 | Speaking with praise |
| 9. Lying | Ephesians 4:25 <br> Zechariah 8:16 | Speaking truth |
| 10. Profanity | Psalm 109:17 <br> 1 Timothy 4:12 | Edification |

| | | |
|---|---|---|
| 11. Idle words | Matthew 12:36<br>Proverbs 21:23 | Bridle the tongue |
| 12. Ingratitude | Romans 1:21<br>Ephesians 5:20 | Thankfulness |
| 13. Impatience | James 1:2–4<br>Hebrews 10:16 | Patience |
| 14. Murmuring | Proverbs 19:3<br>1 Thessalonians 5:8 | Gratefulness |
| 15. Complaining | Jude 15,16<br>Hebrews 13:5 | Contentment |
| 16. Irritation to others | Proverbs 25:8<br>Philippians 2:3,4 | Preferring in love |
| 17. Jealousy | Proverbs 27:4<br>1 Corinthians 13:4 | Trust, preferring others |
| 18. Strife | James 3:16<br>Luke 6:31 | Esteem of others |
| 19. Losing temper | Proverbs 16:32<br>Romans 5:3,4 | Self-Control |
| 20. Complacency | James 4:17<br>Colossians 3:23 | Diligence |

We say that we marry for love, but what type of love? Let's look at three different types of love and their effect upon marriage.

*Eros* is need love. It is the love that leads to marriage. Most couples begin their marriage with a preponderance of eros love and a minimum of the others. Eros is necessary for marriage to succeed. Often it begins in attraction. (Diagram 9.)

After marriage the eros or excitement phase begins to diminish. We need to remember that a marriage cannot be

DIAGRAM 9

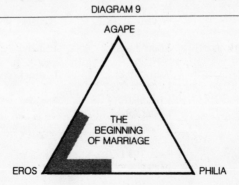

AGAPE

THE BEGINNING OF MARRIAGE

EROS                              PHILIA

sustained by eros alone. Elaine Walster, psychology and sociology professor at the University of Wisconsin, has confirmed the short-lived nature of romantic love. Over the past 15 years Dr. Walster interviewed or observed more than 100,000 persons to study the differences between "passionate" and "compassionate" love. She found that for most couples, intense passion lasts from six months to about two-and-a-half years (see Diagram 10). For love to last it has to move from the eros stage to the level of friendship.

DIAGRAM 10

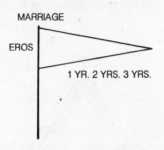

In many marriages *agape* and *philia* remain at a low level and eros recedes. The passion and excitement that were the mortar holding the marriage together initially are no longer there (see Diagram 11). At this point many couples begin to question, "Why am I married? Was I ever in love in the first place?"

DIAGRAM 11

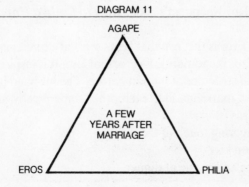

79

But this need not be the pattern for Christian marriages. If individuals would put forth effort to purposely increase philia and agape love, all three types of love would increase (see Diagram 12). The friendship love of philia can enhance and enrich both of the others. The agape love in turn can increase and enhance the others. Both agape and philia can enrich the eros love so it does not have to diminish as much as it usually does. It too can flourish if properly nurtured, and if so, the other types of love are reinforced. But all three must be given conscious effort.

Agape can keep the marriage going when eros and philia are low.

DIAGRAM 12

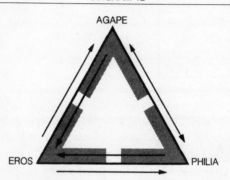

The following material, designed to give practical, day-by-day illustrations of these three types of love, has been taken from LeRoy Koopman's book, *How to Build a Happy Marriage.*[1]

**Eros.** Eros is the love that seeks sensual expression. Eros is desire. Eros is a romantic love, sexual love. It is inspired by the biological structure of human nature. The husband and wife, in a good marriage, love each other romantically and erotically. Eros is:

- the lingering touch of the fingers
- the deep kiss
- candles and music at dinner

80

- the "I promise you" wink
- a low whistle when she models a new dress
- giving her a sheer negligee for her birthday
- wearing it for him the same night

**WHAT DO YOU THINK?**

Can you suggest three more examples of eros love?

1.

2.

3.

**Philia.** In a good marriage the husband and wife are also friends. Friendship means companionship. Philia's companionship is many things:
- being reasonably happy to go shopping with her
- watching TV together and munching popcorn
- feeling lonely when he's out of town

**WHAT DO YOU THINK?**

Name three more manifestations of philia love:

1.

2.

3.

Friendship also means communication. Philia's communication is many things:
- sharing something you read in a book or magazine
- reminiscing how you had to catch all the mice and remove all the bats before you could move into your first apartment
- eating breakfast together without the morning paper
- agreeing on the design of the new wallpaper for Jane's room
- having the courage to tell her you don't like that dress she's trying on

**WHAT DO YOU THINK?**

Suggest three more communication examples:

1.

2.

3.

Philia is also cooperation. While eros is almost always a face-to-face relationship, philia is very often a shoulder-to-shoulder relationship. When there is philia, husband and wife are working together on something greater than both of them. They are finding their oneness, not directly in each other, but in their interest in a common cause. In eros each seeks fulfillment in the other; in philia they both seek fulfillment in one mutual goal.

Philia cooperation is:
- weeding the tomatoes together
- papering the kitchen wall
- working out a new budget with the old income and the new inflation
- washing and drying dishes together

**WHAT DO YOU THINK?**

Suggest three more cooperation ideas:

1.

2.

3.

Here is a quote from another resource to help explain the friendship phase of marriage:

"And what is a friend? Many things . . .

"A friend is someone you are comfortable with, someone whose company you prefer. A friend is someone you can count on—not only for support, but for honesty.

82

"A friend is one who believes in you . . . someone with whom you can share your dreams. In fact, a real friend is a person you want to share all of life with—and the sharing doubles the fun.

"When you are hurting and you can share your struggle with a friend, it eases the pain. A friend offers you safety and trust . . . whatever you say will never be used against you.

"A friend will laugh with you, but not at you . . . a friend is fun.

"A friend will pray with you . . . and for you.

"My friend is one who hears my cry of pain, who senses my struggle, who shares my lows as well as my highs.

"When I am troubled, my friend stands not only by my side, but also stands apart, looking at me with some objectivity. My friend does not always say I am right, because sometimes I am not.

"My lover, my friend—this is what a marriage partner should be."[2]

**Agape.** Agape is self-giving love, gift love, the love that goes on loving even when the other person becomes unlovable. Agape can keep erotic love alive or rekindle erotic love that has been lost. *Agape love is not just something that happens to you; it's something you make happen.* Love is a personal act of commitment. Christ's love (and hence the pattern for our love) is gift love. Christ's love for us is unconditional. Christ's love is eternal love.

Rick Yohn, in *Beyond Spiritual Gifts*, describes how the ancient Greeks used the term *agape*: "[Agape] included the emotions but wasn't limited by them. It included a natural affection, but even when it wasn't natural to love, *agape* loved anyway. This love provided an excellent basis for companionship, but it transcended that phase if the companion failed to love in return.

"When the Bible states that God is love, it uses *agape*.

John wrote, 'God so loved [*agape*] the world, that He gave His only begotten Son' (John 3:16). *Agape* gives. *Agape* sacrifices. *Agape* initiates love. 'We love, because He first loved us' (1 John 4:19). . . .

"*Agape* loves whether or not the object deserves that love. 'But God demonstrates His own love toward us, in that while we were yet sinners, Christ died for us' (Romans 5:8).

"A husband who loves his wife as Christ loved [*agape*] the church will make every sacrifice to meet her needs (not necessarily all her wants). He will provide for her physical needs of sexual love, financial security, clothes, food, etc. He will provide for her emotional needs like security, affection, understanding, acceptance, the feeling of being wanted, and of feeling necessary to complete him. He will provide for her spiritual needs by encouraging her to grow in the Lord. He will set the example of what it means to walk in the Spirit."[3]

Agape is kindness. It is being sympathetic, thoughtful, and sensitive to the needs of your loved one. What is agape kindness? It is:

- being gentle when she burns the toast
- treating his case of the flu as if it were a combination of the eight most awful ailments ever known to mankind
- squelching the urge to ask whether she's been eating more chocolates lately
- listening when she wakes up and wants to talk at 2:35 A.M.
- helping to put the children to bed, even during the fourth quarter of the TV football game

**WHAT DO YOU THINK?**

Suggest three more examples of agape kindness:

1.

2.

3.

Agape kindness is servant power. Kindness is love's willingness to enhance the life of another. It is the readiness to move close to another and allow him/her to move close to you. Agape is trying to be content with those things that don't live up to your expectations.

What is agape contentment? It is:

- learning to live with less than perfection
- not making nostalgic comments about your mother's fine cooking
- using gentle encouragement instead of nagging insistence
- not complaining about eating at McDonald's instead of Caesar's

**WHAT DO YOU THINK?**

Add three more illustrations of agape contentment:

1.

2.

3.

Agape love is forgiving love. What is agape forgiveness? It is forgiving your partner for:

- squeezing the toothpaste tube wrong for the 837th time
- not remembering to pick up Freddy from his guitar lesson
- not having your shirt ironed on time
- having a relative like Uncle Howard

**WHAT DO YOU THINK?**

List three more ways you can show agape forgiveness:

1.

2.

3.

Since agape love is the heart of the marital love relationship, let's think some more about this gift love.

Agape love is a healing force. To demonstrate the power of this love, let's apply it to a critical area that affects marriage—irritability. Irritability is a barrier to need fulfillment. It keeps others at a distance if they know it is present within us. It is the launching pad for attack, lashing out, anger, sharp words, resentment, and refusal of others' offers to love us.

Agape love is unique in that it causes us to seek to meet the needs of our mate rather than demanding that our own needs be reciprocated. Our irritability and frustration diminish because we are seeking to fulfill another rather than pursuing and demanding our own need satisfaction.

Lewis B. Smedes, in his excellent work *Love Within Limits*, describes the effect of agape love: "Agape love reduces irritability because this love meets our deepest need. As God reaches down to us with His immense gift of eternal life we experience this agape love coming from Him."[4] This act enables us to move toward others with love.

We read in 1 John 4:7,9,14–16,19: "Beloved, let us love one another, for love is from God; and every one who loves is born of God and knows God. . . .By this the love of God was manifested in us, that God has sent His only begotten Son into the world so that we might live through Him. . . . And we have beheld and bear witness that the Father has sent the Son to be the Savior of the world. Whoever confesses that Jesus is the Son of God, God abides in him, and he in God. And we have come to know and have believed the love which God has for us. God is love, and the one who abides in love abides in God, and God abides in him. . . .We love, because He first loved us" (*NASB*).

This love can reduce the potential for frustration. Striving for self-satisfaction breeds frustration, but because God has met our basic needs for love, assurance, security, and self-worth, we are no longer chained to the bondage of self-satisfaction. This freedom gives us patience in our relationship with our spouse. Our frustration level drops significantly when we are concerned with others, and therefore the potential for anger is lessened.

Our agape love can increase our gratitudes as well with constant awareness and remembrance of God's agape love for us. An attitude of thankfulness for all of life develops. We are able to see and concentrate upon the positive qualities and attributes of our spouse, which we may overlook or take for granted. Our mind-set and attitudes can be refocused because of the presence of agape love. Our attitudes of appreciation cause us to respond with even more love toward our spouses.

Agape love manifests itself with these characteristics. It is an *unconditional love*. It is not based upon the spouse's performance, but upon our need to share this act with our spouse. If we don't, he may live with the fear that we will limit our love if he does not meet our expectations. Our agape love is in spite of how he or she behaves. Real love is an unconditional commitment to an imperfect person.

Agape love is also a transparent love. It is strong enough to allow our partner to get close to us and inside us. Transparency involves honesty, truth, and sharing positive and negative feelings.

Paul Tournier shared the story of a woman whose mother gave her this advice: "Don't tell your husband everything: to maintain her prestige and keep her husband's love, a woman must retain a certain mystery for him." Tournier commented, "What a mistake! It fails to recognize the meaning of marriage and the meaning of love. Transparency is the law of marriage and the couple must strive for it untiringly at the cost of confessions which are always new and sometimes very hard."[5]

Agape love has a deep reservoir to draw from, so no matter what occurs the love is felt and provides stability during times of stress and conflict.

1. List five additional manifestations of agape love that you feel your spouse would enjoy.

(1)                                      (4)

(2)                                      (5)

(3)

2. When your spouse is having a down day, is disappointed or depressed, what can you do to support and help him/her at this time?

3. If you find that your life reflects more negative behaviors than positive ones, how should you proceed? Would you try to reduce the negative behaviors so that the positive ones have an opportunity to exist? Yes ☐ No ☐

There are many who take this approach. But consider this alternative. If a husband or wife attempted to increase his positive behaviors and demonstrate as many of them as possible each day, he soon would crowd out the negative behaviors and responses. Negative behaviors are chased away by the positive as the benefits for the giver and receiver are more need fulfilling.

## Notes

1. LeRoy Koopman, *How to Build a Happy Marriage* (Grand Rapids: Baker Book House, 1976), pp. 4–23.
2. Lou and Colleen Evans, *My Lover, My Friend* (Old Tappan, N.J.: Revell, 1976), pp. 121,122.
3. Rick Yohn, *Beyond Spiritual Gifts* (Wheaton, IL: Tyndale House, 1976), pp. 27,28.
4. Lewis B. Smedes, *Love Within Limits* (Grand Rapids: Wm. B. Eerdmans Publishing Co., 1978), p. 63.
5. Paul Tournier, *Secrets* (Richmond, VA: John Knox Press, 1965), p. 50.

## CHAPTER SEVEN

# MARITAL CHANGE AND STRESS

We are in a constant state of change. Our bodies change, our beliefs change, our physical abilities change, and life around us changes. Most of us say that we're all for change, but are we really? We may like change if we can be in control, but we may resist unexpected or traumatic change. We often resist planned, positive changes in our life because the adjustment we are called upon to make may require more energy than we are willing to invest.

Your marriage relationship will change too. All marriages enter into phases or stages. The changes that occur in these stages are not necessarily good or bad, but they are reality. Here are the typical stages through which most marriages pass:

1. Honeymoon
2. Expectant parenthood
3. Parenthood with preschool children
4. Child rearing
5. Parenthood with adolescents
6. Child launching

7. Empty nest
8. Retirement

Often we are not equipped or prepared to face the changes. Ignoring the inevitable and refusing to think about (and plan for) these changes make adjustment to them even more difficult.

Our roles in life change, and the tasks involved in maintaining our home, family, and job change as well. The changes around us cause us to change as individuals, and our relationships with others, such as our spouse and children, begin to change as well.

Some changes come upon us without warning or choice on our part, but there are some changes that we can control by choice. We can choose not to plan changes for our marriage. We may want to keep it as it is. If changes do occur, they will have to come without any effort on our part. This choice is made with the attitude that if we do nothing, our marriage will change naturally and for the better. If our marriage does not change for the better, we can always blame our spouse. Couples who choose not to plan changes assume that change must occur outside of themselves.

Some couples choose to change their relationship by distance; they separate or divorce. Often this change comes when the couple believes that the other person is responsible for the trouble in the marriage. Like couples who do not plan changes, couples who create distance between themselves assume that change must occur outside of themselves.

Marital change also occurs by choice. An internal change on our part provides a basis for marital change. Personal responsibility creates the conditions for change. The first two choices—failure to plan for changes and the creating of distance—cannot bring about a positive change in a marital relationship. Luciano and Bess L'Abate explain why not:

"Our marriage will not change unless we both desire it and recognize our helplessness to do anything constructive about

90

it without our partner's help. Change starts in our recognition of helplessness in ourselves. We cannot change the world (although we may try), we cannot change our mate (and we may try). We can only change ourselves (which is very hard), while changing others is impossible."[1]

We need to expect change in marriage, say David and Vera Mace: "We need to see marriage in new terms, as a continually growing, continually changing, interaction between a man and woman who are seeking the warmth and richness of the shared life. Marriage has too often been portrayed as two people frozen together side by side, as immobile as marble statues. More accurately, it is the intricate and graceful cooperation of two dancers who through long practice have learned to match each other's movements and moods in response to the music of the spheres."[2]

Three factors that will bring about change are commitment, communication, and strength. If change is going to occur, both partners need to be committed to this goal. Their mutual commitment allows them to invest their energy in changing the marriage. Change can occur if a couple is willing to talk over every concern. Care and love are reflected through this willingness.

This type of communication will build what has been called "flexible trust." Static trust is a rigid, locked-in system in which each person's behavior is so predictable and routine that the relationship's stability is based upon openness and honesty in all types of circumstances so that you can "count on" the other person, even in changing circumstances. The more open two people are, the greater the trust, for the fear of deception is absent.[3]

A strong person is the kind of individual who wants to change. A weak person does not admit the need to change nor does he ask for help. He may feel the pain of despair, but he equates doing something about it as an admission of weakness—thus the refusal.

Are you the kind of person who changes easily? Do you desire change? Evaluate yourself with these questions:

1. List a change that you have made in each of the following areas during the past year:

(1) attitude:

(2) values:

(3) behavior:

2. Which of the following have changed in the past three years (check):

☐ the time you arise in the morning?
☐ the time you retire in the evening?
☐ the time you have meals?
☐ the way you greet your spouse at the end of the day?
☐ the type of food you eat?
☐ the way you perform your daily tasks?
☐ the way you make marital decisions?
☐ the way you and your spouse communicate?
☐ the way you express your love sexually?
☐ the way you pray?

3. What three positive changes would you like to make in your own life?

4. What three positive changes would your spouse like to make in his life?

5. What three positive changes would both of you like to make in your marriage?

---

While some changes in our environment or life situation are neither good nor bad, too many changes all at once could affect us in an adverse way. Such changes are referred to as stress. We have all experienced stress. If you have ever had an auto accident, made someone upset, or been asked to speak before a large group, you have experienced stress.

Stress can be useful and necessary. Many great human achievements have been accomplished under stress. Sometimes God uses stress in our life to refine us. But stress can also be dangerous if there is too much in too brief a time span.

Many doctors in the medical field are concerned about the effects of stress because too much adrenaline in our system too often (the hormone activated by stress) could affect us adversely. Even too many changes too fast may tax our resources for handling these changes. In attempting to evaluate the effects of change, two medical doctors devised a stress test.[4] Read through the test and complete the evaluation (Diagram 13). When you are finished, add up the total number of points.

DIAGRAM 13

## HOLMES-RAHE STRESS TEST

In the past 12 months, which of these have happened to you?

| EVENT | VALUE | SCORE |
|-------|-------|-------|
| Death of spouse | 100 | |
| Divorce | 73 | |
| Marital separation | 65 | |

Jail term . . . . . . . . . . . . . . . . . . . . . . . . . . . 63 _____

Death of close family member . . . . . . . . . . . . 63 _____

Personal injury or illness . . . . . . . . . . . . . . . . 53 _____

Marriage . . . . . . . . . . . . . . . . . . . . . . . . . . . 50 _____

Fired from work . . . . . . . . . . . . . . . . . . . . . . 47 _____

Marital reconciliation . . . . . . . . . . . . . . . . . . . 45 _____

Retirement . . . . . . . . . . . . . . . . . . . . . . . . . . 45 _____

Change in family member's health . . . . . . . . . . 44 _____

Pregnancy . . . . . . . . . . . . . . . . . . . . . . . . . . 40 _____

Sex difficulties . . . . . . . . . . . . . . . . . . . . . . . 39 _____

Addition to family . . . . . . . . . . . . . . . . . . . . . 39 _____

Business readjustment . . . . . . . . . . . . . . . . . . 39 _____

Change in financial status . . . . . . . . . . . . . . . 38 _____

Death of close friend . . . . . . . . . . . . . . . . . . . 37 _____

Change in number of marital arguments . . . . . 35 _____

Mortgage or loan over $10,000 . . . . . . . . . . . 31 _____

Foreclosure of mortgage or loan . . . . . . . . . . 30 _____

Change in work responsibilities . . . . . . . . . . . 29 _____

Son or daughter leaving home . . . . . . . . . . . . 29 _____

Trouble with in-laws . . . . . . . . . . . . . . . . . . . 29 _____

Outstanding personal achievement . . . . . . . . . 28 _____

Spouse begins or starts work . . . . . . . . . . . . . 26 _____

Starting or finishing school . . . . . . . . . . . . . . . 26 _____

Change in living conditions . . . . . . . . . . . . . . . 25 _____

Revision of personal habits . . . . . . . . . . . . . . . 24 _____

Trouble with boss . . . . . . . . . . . . . . . . . . . . . 23 _____

Change in work hours, conditions . . . . . . . . . . 20 _____

Change in residence . . . . . . . . . . . . . . . . . . . 20 _____

Change in schools . . . . . . . . . . . . . . . . . . . . . 20 _____

Change in recreational habits . . . . . . . . . . . . . 19 _____

Change in church activities . . . . . . . . . . . . . . . 19 _____

Change in social activities . . . . . . . . . . . . . . . 18 _____

Mortgage or loan under $10,000 . . . . . . . . . . 18 _____

Change in sleeping habits . . . . . . . . . . . . . . . 16 _____

Change in number of family gatherings . . . . . . 15 _____

Change in eating habits . . . . . . . . . . . . . . . . . 15 _____

Vacation . . . . . . . . . . . . . . . . . . . . . . . . . . . 13 _____

Christmas season . . . . . . . . . . . . . . . . . . . . . 12 _____

Minor violation of the law . . . . . . . . . . . . . . . . 11 _____

TOTAL                                    _____

According to the two doctors who devised this test, Holmes and Rahe, if your score is under 150 stress units, you have only a 37-percent chance of being sick within the next two years. If your score is between 150 and 300, the probability rises to 51 percent. And if your score is over 300, the odds are four to five (80 percent) that you will be sick during the next two years. The predicted sickness could be a physical illness or depression. Depression following a major change in life-style is quite common. This test is widely used, especially in the military, to predict whether one will be sick during the subsequent two years.

Stress is neither good nor bad (note the several positive events on the stress test)—how a person reacts to it makes the difference. You can grow and master a situation, or you can allow it to affect you emotionally and physically. Here are 10 potential causes of stress. Do any of them fit you?

1. *An unresolved relationship.* If you have uncertainties about your marriage, such as wondering if your partner is unhappy or if he is thinking of leaving you, stress is present. This type of burden can color your attitude toward all other areas of life (see Phil. 4:6,7).

2. *Your environment* can contribute to your stress. A monotonous and repetitious environment can be just as much a problem as a fast-paced, pressure-filled, competitive atmosphere (see John 16:33).

3. *Perfectionism.* Having excessively high standards is a way to set oneself up for failure and self-rejection. A perfectionistic husband or wife is often hard to live with too! No one is or can be perfect. The only perfect and sinless person ever to have lived was Jesus Christ.

Perfectionism can also mean insecurity. Secure people are flexible and are willing to take risks and make positive changes. When we have unrealistic expectations and don't live up to them, we begin to despise ourselves, which can lead to depression (see 1 John 4:7).

4. *Impatience.* If you are impatient with others, you are probably impatient with yourself. Not seeing or getting things done according to your schedule keeps your insides in a turmoil. The word *patience* means forbearance, not hasty or impulsive, steadfast, able to bear (see Gal. 5:22,23).

5. *Rigidity* can be closely tied to perfectionism and impatience. Rigid people spend their time prospecting for something to be upset over. The admission of error or acceptance of another's opinion is a mature and stress-reducing response. Ephesians 4:2 could be a corrective if put into practice "making allowances because you love one another" (*AMP*).

6. *Inability to relax.* Can you sit in a chair for 10 minutes and totally relax? Does your mind keep running over everything you feel you need to do? Do you constantly push yourself and hurry your pace? If so, your activity is called stress momentum (see Isa. 32:17).

7. *Explosiveness and anger.* If your life is characterized by bombs spreading angry shrapnel at others, stress is not only affecting you but others. Expressing anger is better than bottling it up, but continual outbursts are not healthy (see Prov. 29:22).

8. *Lack of humor and little enthusiasm.* People who are filled with self-conceit, self-reproach, and therefore stress, are probably depressed as well (see Phil. 4:13).

9. *Too much competition.* Comparing ourself with others in terms of what they do and what they have, places unneeded pressure on ourselves. Why should what others do and have affect our state of mind? Some competition in certain areas can be fun and enjoyable, but when it's constant, it's no fun (see Ps. 37:3).

10. *Lack of self-worth.* A low self-concept is the basis for many of our difficulties. Depression or stress can occur. If you lack importance or influence in your marriage, you may have encouraged your spouse or other family members to treat you in such a way that this feeling is reinforced (see Ps. 8:4,5).

Let's evaluate stress in your life.

1. During the last five years of your marriage, when have you experienced the greatest amount of stress, and what contributed to this stress?

| TIME | CAUSE |
|------|-------|
| Present to 1 year ago | |
| 1–2 years ago | |
| 2–3 years ago | |
| 3–4 years ago | |
| 4–5 years ago | |

2. During the last five years of your marriage, when has your spouse experienced the greatest amount of stress, and what contributed to his stress?

| TIME | CAUSE |
|------|-------|
| Present to 1 year ago | |
| 1–2 years ago | |
| 2–3 years ago | |
| 3–4 years ago | |
| 4–5 years ago | |

3. Indicate which of these 10 possible causes of stress, if any, could be creating stress for you (underline):

(1) An unresolved relationship

(2) Environment

(3) Perfectionism

(4) Impatience

(5) Rigidity

(6) Inability to relax

(7) Explosiveness and anger

(8) Lack of humor and little enthusiasm

(9) Too much competition

(10) Lack of self-worth

4. Now evaluate your marriage using the following questions:
(1) What aspects of your marriage have created stress?


(2) How has your spouse helped you handle stress?


(3) Are there any outside stresses affecting your marriage at the present time? If so, what are they?

---

What can you do about stress? Remember that stress comes from the choices we make and from our attitude toward life situations. God is aware of our stresses, and we are not alone. Even the apostle Paul experienced stress. He described some of his stressful experiences:

"Five times I received from the Jews thirty-nine lashes. Three times I was beaten with rods, once I was stoned, three times I was shipwrecked, a night and a day I have spent in the deep. I have been on frequent journeys, in dangers from rivers, dangers from robbers, dangers from my countrymen, dangers from the Gentiles, dangers in the city, dangers in the wilderness, dangers on the sea, dangers among false brethren; I have been in labor and hardship, through many sleepless nights, in hunger and thirst, often without food, in cold and exposure. Apart from such external things, there is the daily pressure upon me of concern for all the churches" (2 Cor. 11:24–28, *NASB*).

"In addition to all of this, Paul had a 'thorn in the flesh.' Three times he asked God to take it away, but when it persisted the Apostle concluded that it was keeping him humble and enabling him to grow spiritually (2 Corinthians 12:7–10). From these and other verses in the Bible we get the impression that Paul tried to see the positive side of his stresses and used them as growing experiences."[5]

"We are pressed on every side by troubles, but not crushed and broken. We are perplexed because we don't know why things happen as they do, but we don't give up and quit. We are hunted down, but God never abandons us. We get knocked down, but we get up again and keep going. These bodies of ours are constantly facing death just as Jesus did; so it is clear to all that it is only the living Christ within [who keeps us safe].

"Yes, we live under constant danger to our lives because we serve the Lord, but this gives us constant opportunities to show forth the power of Jesus Christ within our dying bodies. Because of our preaching we face death, but it has resulted in eternal life for you" (2 Cor. 4:8–12, *TLB*).

"Paul knew that he could overcome his stresses, but he also realized that stress could cause people to go down spiritually. It had caused John Mark to give up the ministry. Demas forsook the faith because of a love for the world, and even Paul himself seemed to be struggling with the stress of loneliness in the last letter he wrote to Timothy (2 Timothy 4:9–21).

"Most of us discover that stress can have one of two influences on our relationship with God: it can draw us closer, or it can cause us to turn away in bitterness and disappointment. For some of us we even vacillate, alternating between prayer and an angry, frustrated rejection of spiritual things."[6]

Here are several suggestions that can help you with stress in and outside of your marriage relationship:

When you are upset or have experienced a loss, *openly express your feelings*. They must be released, and crying or talking can be very beneficial. We cannot carry our burdens alone, and we don't have to. Share with your spouse or other members of the Body of Christ.

*Engage in some type of physical activity* that will drain

out energy and stress and assist you in relaxing. Many Christians are concerned about not abusing their bodies as temples of the Holy Spirit by not smoking or using certain beverages or food, but our bodies can be just as abused by lack of use!

When you find your mind working overtime and you begin to pressure yourself and experience anxiety through your thoughts, *begin the practice of thought control.* Scripture teaches that thought control is possible. It takes the work of the Holy Spirit and our efforts to do it.

Paul said: "Do not be conformed to this world, but be transformed by the renewing of your mind" (Rom. 12:2, *NASB*). Paul was talking about a renovation, a complete change for the better. The word *renew* actually means "to make new from above." Man's thoughts, imaginations, and reasoning are changed through the working of the Holy Spirit.

Powerful as the Holy Spirit is, He cannot do the job alone. He requires your cooperation. You must be aware of the scriptural teaching that the Holy Spirit will empower you. Then you must act on that awareness by saying, "I no longer have to be controlled by my own thoughts; I have power made available to me. I'm going to let the Holy Spirit assist me in controlling my mind. No longer can I say, 'I cannot control my thoughts,' because the Scriptures say I can."

Many people think that relying upon the Holy Spirit means sitting back and saying, "Well, I'll just let Him do it; I don't need to put forth any effort." The Scriptures do not teach that; they teach that we have a very definite responsibility in the process of controlling our thoughts. First Peter 1:13 says to "gird up your minds" (*RSV*). *Gird* actually means "mental exertion." As a Christian, you and I are to put out of our thoughts anything that will hinder our Christian development, our relationship with the Lord.[7]

*Get rid of "hurry ups"*—slow down your driving, eating, shopping, and talking. Force yourself to perform some of your activities and tasks at a much slower pace. Purposely choose to do something you want to do, but leisurely.

*Eliminate what "deadlines" you can.* Many are self-imposed, and regulation can be too severe. Ask yourself the reason for the deadlines. Is it really necessary? Too often once you reach a deadline, you just create another.

*Redo your expectations for yourself in all phases of your life.* Select tasks and jobs that are manageable. If your self-concept is built upon your performance or expectations, you will feel good about yourself. Challenge some of those "oughts" and "shoulds" that you have in your life.

A suggestion made by Dr. Ahlem is to *avoid the "magic of the mouth" symptom*, which can occur because of stress and contribute to the stress. Excessive eating, drinking, smoking, and talking is a sign of poor coping. Keeping impulses under control is a sign of healthy coping.[8]

## WHAT'S YOUR PLAN?

1. If you could eliminate one factor from your life right now that you feel is producing stress, what would it be?


2. If you could not eliminate this factor, what could you do to lessen its effect?


3. What three passages of Scripture, if applied to your life, could help you handle frustration?

## Notes

1. Luciano and Bess L'Abate, *How to Avoid Divorce* (Atlanta: John Knox Press, 1977), p. 58.
2. David and Vera Mace, *We Can Have Better Marriages if We Really Want Them* (Nashville: Abingdon, 1974), p. 9.
3. Adapted from Marcia Lasswell and Norman Lobsenz, *No Fault Marriage* (New York: Ballantine Books, 1976), p. 144.
4. Thomas H. Holmes and Richard Rahe, Stress Rating Scale, *Journal of Psychosomatic Research,* 1967, vol. 2, p. 216. Used by permission.
5. Gary Collins, *You Can Profit from Stress* (Santa Ana, CA: Vision House Publishers, 1978), pp. 32,33.
6. Collins, p. 33.
7. Comments on thought control are adapted from H. Norman Wright, *An Answer to Anxiety* (Irvine, CA: Harvest House, 1976), pp. 50,51.
8. See Lloyd H. Ahlem, *How to Cope with Conflict, Crisis and Change* (Glendale, CA: Regal Books, 1978), pp. 149.

## CHAPTER EIGHT

# COPING WITH
# MAJOR CRISES

In addition to the stress-producing changes that occur in the various stages of marriage, events occur in our environment that also produce stress. A 1971 issue of *Science Digest* reported a study by Eugene S. Pakyel in which 373 people were asked to rate the most "upsetting" events *in their life.* The 25 most distressing events (which can induce a depressive reaction), from most stressful to least stressful, were:

1. Death of a child
2. Death of a spouse
3. Jail sentence
4. Unfaithful spouse
5. Major financial difficulty
6. Business failure
7. Being fired
8. Miscarriage or stillbirth
9. Divorce
10. Marital separation due to an argument
11. Court appearance
12. Unwanted pregnancy
13. Major illness in the family
14. Unemployment for a month (additional studies indicated that four out of five marriages end in divorce when the husband is out of work for nine months or more)

15. Death of a close friend
16. Demotion
17. Major personal illness
18. Start of an extramarital affair
19. Loss of personally valued objects
20. Lawsuit
21. Academic failure
22. Child married without family approval
23. Broken engagement
24. Taking out a large loan
25. Son drafted[1]

Many changes can be planned for in advance and their intensity can be lessened. Sudden changes, however, can throw us—a person loses his job, a promotion falls through, a spouse becomes ill, a child is born with a defect, a death occurs in the family, a parent moves in.

According to family service experts, "Any sudden change becomes a threat to whatever marital balance has been achieved. It tends to reawaken personal insecurities that the marriage has successfully overcome or held in check. You've noticed how sick people tend to fall back into childish ways—they become terribly dependent, demanding, unreasonable. Similarly, some people regress in other kinds of emotional crises. Long-conquered patterns of behavior reassert themselves, at least until the first impact of the shock has been absorbed."[2]

One of the most critical elements that helps a marriage survive a sudden crisis is the emotional interdependence between the partners. Without this interdependence a sudden upset from the outside can be crippling. Marriages that are strong emotionally tend to become stronger in a crisis. Those that are weak become weaker.

Let's consider a few events that may become crises.

*Loss of a job.* When a man loses a job and remains unemployed for a considerable amount of time, a marriage can be disrupted. If his wife has never been employed, the role reversal can be uncomfortable. If the couple has been avoiding conflict issues, the husband's increased presence around the house can force more conflicts. Many men's self-concept is related to their involvement at work, and thus losing a job is a severe blow. Losing his job may lead a man to overemphasize his authority at home. This is a time when balanced emotional support and honest communication can be a healing influence.

*Birth of a child.* The birth of a child can affect both partners unless time and effort have gone into the planning necessary to be parents. Unfortunately, most couples do not plan for the birth of a child. Some husbands become upset by the new expectations placed upon them: less attention from their wives, less sleep and rest, perhaps more work around the house, and less spontaneous availability of their wives to go out or entertain.

Many mothers become depressed after the birth of a child. Their depression is called the "four-day blues" or postpartum blues. Many husbands have difficulty handling this kind of depression because they cannot understand why it occurs. Hormonal disturbances or drugs that the woman has taken could contribute to this depression. Physical exhaustion could also be a contributing factor.

A woman who is a perfectionist may have difficulty adjusting to the arrival of a noisy, dirty, and demanding child. She would like to be the perfect mother with the perfect child and finds coping with reality difficult. Perhaps the wife has had an idealized picture of what having a child would be like, and the responsibility begins to weigh heavily upon her. Now that she has a home, a husband, and a child, she may begin to question her ability to handle all of these responsibilities. All of these new responsibilities, coupled with uncertainty, may also bring about a change in her self-concept.

Another reason for a prolonged postpartum depression

may be that she thinks a mother should feel pride and satisfaction at the birth of a healthy child, and when she does not, she begins to question herself and consider herself a failure or a poor mother. Many life changes occur at this time!

*Moving to a new community.* Financial strain, selling, renting, redecorating, excessive physical energy expended, loss of familiar surroundings, new schools, new church, and new friends are all involved when a family moves to a new community.

*Spouse's illness.* A spouse's illness can seriously affect the emotional balance of a marriage. If a husband is sick, his wife may feel threatened with the potential emotional and/or financial loss. Again, some dormant conflicts may emerge. If a child is ill, parents become frightened, which causes anxiety for them. Illness can create strain upon the marriage.

*Death of a child.* A prevailing assumption is that a couple who loses a child through death draws closer together in their marital relationship. Statistics indicate, however, that the effect of the child's death on the marriage is usually negative.

" 'An astonishing seventy percent of marriages, where children have been lost, become endangered and end in separation or divorce,' is the claim of Compassionate Friends, an eight-year-old self-help organization of bereaved parents. Founded by an Anglican priest, the Reverend Simon Stephens, the society has given such parents the chance to meet together, talk, and if need be, cry together unashamedly, in the hope that grief shared with others who understand is thereby lessened.

" 'Most people are under the false impression that couples get closer after they lose a child. Not true. Most of the marriages go bad,' said Ernie and Joyce Friereich of Commack, New York, founders of a New York Chapter of Compassionate Friends.

"Harriet Schiff, author of a new book called *The Bereaved Parent* (Crown, 1977), puts the marriage break-up figure

106

even higher than does Compassionate Friends. She states, 'Some studies estimate that as high as ninety percent of all bereaved couples are in serious marital difficulty within months after the death of their child.' "[3]

Why should this happen? The pain of losing a child is more intense for a number of reasons. Parents are often confused by the reality posed in the question, How can a parent outlive his child? A loss of anticipation for the future is experienced by the parents to an intense degree when a child dies. Harriet Schiff spoke of it in this way:

"To bury a child is to see part of yourself, your eye color, your dimple, your sense of humor, being placed in the ground. It is life's harshest empathetic experience and must therefore be the hardest one with which to deal. In reality, when children die, not only are we mourning them, we are also mourning that bit of our own immortality that they carried."[4]

Grief in this loss is more intense and goes on for years and years. It is extremely persistent. The "if only" question haunts many parents and provokes guilt—"If only I had done something different, our child would be alive." The parent blames both himself and his partner. If parents have watched a child die slowly, an intense pressure is constantly present.

If parents fail to work through the grief process and their grief is unresolved, it turns inward and becomes destructive. As a husband and wife struggle with their hurt, pain, and depression, each has little to give to the other. Antoinette Bosco described the problem:

"The result is a strained marriage, with two people unable to function in a relationship requiring a high degree of need-satisfaction, mutual help and understanding concern for the other. The marriage situation becomes a couple divided into two singles, each attempting to survive personally in an environment of co-existence rather than covenant or community, each feeling the shock waves of learning that suffering is such a very individual condition."[5]

Other problems include conflict over how to remember the child. What should we do with his belongings? Should we keep his picture around? Often parents deny themselves pleasure at this time. One of the most common denials is sexual relations. Perhaps this area of denial reminds them too much of how the child came into existence.

Marriages do not have to die when a child dies. In the midst of intense pain and loss, it is possible to reach out to each other. They have to *choose* to live again, to activate their faith and share their pain with the Lord. Through this experience the word of God can help parents gradually hope again. The awareness and application of "My grace is sufficient for thee" will become evident in time. If you know couples who have lost a child, they need your love, concern, listening ear, and support. They will need this support for months and maybe even years. (For additional information, see *The Bereaved Parent* by Harriet Schiff [Crown] and *The View from the Hearse* by Joe Bailey [David C. Cook]).

*Child leaving home.* A child leaving home changes the balance and roles of the family. If you have three children and now only two are left at home, how does this vacancy affect those who remain? What if he was the tension reliever, the joker and humorist? Who picks up the slack?

What happens when the last child leaves the nest? Is this a time of sadness, emptiness? Many marriages dissolve at this point because the couple must face the emptiness of their marriage, which they have been avoiding. But many couples look forward to the time when the last fledgling leaves the nest and enjoy their marriage even more. What makes the difference?

The preceding changes are considered major crises. But for some individuals, even minor changes are major upsets. How would you react if:

- Your spouse no longer ate dinner with you in the evening?

- Your spouse no longer wanted to go to your regular place for dinner?
- Your spouse wanted to change a regular family tradition that includes your parents?
- Your spouse announced that a new business opportunity had opened in another state and wanted to move?
- Your spouse quit preparing your favorite dinner?
- Your spouse changed his/her entire style of clothing?
- You lost $500 investment in a new business through a business reversal?
- Your spouse got rid of your favorite piece of furniture?

## WHAT DO YOU THINK?

1. What minor changes might your spouse make that would surprise you?

2. How would you feel and what would you do?

When a change or crisis occurs, we learn to adapt. We cut loose from our old patterns and, in a sense, come into a new life. This process of adaptation was described by Lloyd Ahlem as a form of death, then new life, and then resurrection:

"The death and resurrection theme seems to describe all

kinds of normal changes in life. Even vacations that alter life significantly seem to have this character. The first few days away from home seem like a stunning mental episode. Then follows a period of depression, until the vacationer arrives back at work just in time to resurrect. Whenever we find ourselves in highly unfamiliar circumstances or under unusual conditions we experience a sense of loss—even when the conditions are those surrounding an event commonly regarded as positive.

"A job promotion, a marriage reconciliation, a move to another geographic location—all these can be essentially positive events that trip off the crisis adaptations in us.

"Another example of the death and resurrection theme may be found in marriage. A wedding is one of the great happy events of life. The bride and groom are almost giddy with joy. They are so preoccupied with each other and because of their happiness they can hardly think straight—and sometimes that's the way they act. It is as though nothing in the world mattered but this great event. And for them that may be true.

"A few months or a year may lapse before they speak objectively about their emotions. But if they are honest, they will often report that the cycle of death and resurrection was present in their emotions. They will inform you that the marriage with all its preparation formed a high moment—so high all else seemed insignificant. Then, beginning a few days or weeks later, their feelings began to die down. They began finding out the realities about each other. Bad breath, annoying habits, dull moments, and in-laws came to their attention. The facades so carefully constructed through romantic days wilted and real people walked out into full view. And it was downright depressing. But then the resurrection began and a normal life-style returned with new joys and new responsibilities.

"The point of these illustrations is that in all of the great changes in our lives, whether in crisis or in death, or in great success and elation, the adaptive responses of people follow essentially the same pattern."[6]

Every life-changing crisis has four phases: (1) impact, (2) withdrawal and confusion, (3) adjustment, and (4) reconstruction and resurrection. An understanding and awareness of these phases will help us in handling crises when they occur, which in turn allow the marriage to be affected positively rather than negatively. Each person is aware of what his partner is experiencing, and the one least affected can be supportive to the other.

*The impact phase* usually is quite brief. This phase begins when the crisis becomes known and we may be stunned. It could last a few hours to a few days. During this phase making decisions is a bit difficult, yet a person must make the fight-or-flight decision at this time. This decision is the question of staying and doing battle with the problem or running and ignoring it. During this phase people usually, in some way, make an attempt to search for what has been lost. Letting go is difficult for many of us, for it means losing control. Much of our security can be based upon being in control of our life, our situation, and events around us. Many have never really learned the meaning of trusting God and allowing Him to control and direct them. Even when a change involves a loss of something or someone who is detrimental to us, we still continue to search.

Often the loss we experience is overemphasized because we have attached too much importance to the object or position. If our loss is extreme, how would the following passages describe us?

"Every tree that does not bear good fruit is cut down, and thrown into the fire. So then, you will know them by their fruits. Not every one who says to Me, Lord, Lord, will enter the kingdom of heaven; but he who does the will of My Father, who is in heaven" (Matt. 7:19–21, *NASB*).

"And the rain descended, and the floods came, and the winds blew, and burst against that house; and yet it did not fall; for it had been founded upon the rock" (Matt. 7:25, *NASB*).

Guilt accompanies change in our life, whether it is a change for the worse or for the better. This occurs because we tend to blame ourselves for the loss or change.

*The second phase is withdrawal and confusion.* The emotional level of a person in crisis drops to almost nothing. He suffers a numbness or depression—a worn-out feeling— which can last for days or even weeks. Many deny their feelings at this time because being angry might lead to guilt or shame. Too often Christians do not accept their capacity for feelings and emotions as a gift from God! This is a time to fully express these emotions. During this time a person must accomplish a detachment from the lost objects. The loss of a possession, job, location, loved one, status, or a change in schedule needs the process of detachment.

*The third phase is adjustment.* Insight begins to emerge and positive attitudes develop. Some depression remains, but optimism is coming back. Detachment from the old is completed, and a search for the new has begun. Often at this time a person says that what he has learned through this experience he would never trade in spite of pain.

*The final phase is reconstruction and reconciliation.* In this stage the person has chosen between self-pity and hope. He establishes reattachments such as a new friend, activity, home, job, hobby, church. Second Corinthians 5:17 is a reality both spiritually and in the area of loss. Reconciliation is usually involved, for when crisis occurs, people around us are often hurt. When we go through a crisis we have a tendency to victimize others. Others feel our stress. Through confession or helpful gestures reconciliation can be accomplished.

The change in a person's emotional level during the four phases of life-changing crises can be seen in Diagram 14.

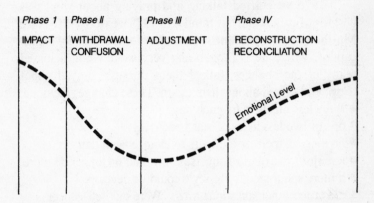

DIAGRAM 14

## CHANGE AND CRISIS SEQUENCE[7]

| Phase 1 | Phase II | Phase III | Phase IV |
|---------|----------|-----------|----------|
| IMPACT | WITHDRAWAL CONFUSION | ADJUSTMENT | RECONSTRUCTION RECONCILIATION |

*Emotional Level*

Is there any way to lessen the intensity of this process so that we suffer less? Yes there is.

First, be aware of the normality of this process. Awareness can relieve some anxiety and guilt for feeling and behaving the way we do.

Second, develop greater flexibility in your daily life-style. Learning to make and accept even minor changes can be a foundation for making larger adjustments.

Third, when major changes are forthcoming, plan for them in advance and learn to rely upon the promises of God's Word.

Just recently our family went through a change and crisis sequence. A few months after our son Matthew was born in 1967, we became aware that his development was quite slow. At eight months of age he began having grand mal seizures. Within a few months we discovered that Matthew had an improper brain formation in addition to brain damage. Since then he was diagnosed as profoundly retarded. He currently functions at a nine-month-old level.

Matthew's presence brought numerous changes and adjustments to all of us. We experienced grief and went through the stages of a severe loss. Joyce and I grew individually in maturity, and our Christian life and our marriage were strengthened.

In 1975 we started talking and praying about what was best for Matthew and our family. In 1978 we were led to place Matthew in a private Christian facility for the severely handicapped, where he is progressing very well. We anticipated many of the changes, talked them through, prayed about them, and talked about them again. These changes included:

- three less meals to fix each day
- one or two less loads of wash each day
- no more diapers or Pampers to change each day
- a major topic of our conversation would no longer be there
- a more spontaneous life-style could be developed

But then other questions arose. Were our self-concepts or feelings about ourselves based on our caring for Matthew? If so, how would placing him in a home affect us? Had we used Matthew in some way to strengthen our feelings of worth? How would we feel about having someone else take care of him and perhaps do a better job? What if he becomes attached to the people at the home more than to us, and what if he forgets us? Were we really doing the right thing for Matthew or was it more for us? Would there be guilt? Did we like having a person be totally dependent upon us?

These were questions that we anticipated and worked through. We also were reminded of God's faithfulness in the past and realized that this too was a step of faith. Our adjustment (which included a time of loss, loneliness, and hurt) was much easier because we planned, prayed, and watched as God continued to work in His unique manner. Prior to Matthew's entering his new home, we scheduled four different dates for the move. Each time there was a delay, because Matthew was sick or because there was a funding problem or a change at the home. When Matthew finally entered the home, the transition was very smooth, since on previous occasions we had already gone through the emotional transition of having everything ready and being prepared for the move. We have learned the truth of God's Word: "Thou dost keep him in perfect peace, whose mind is stayed on thee, because he trusts in thee" (Isa. 26:3, *RSV*).

"But now thus says the Lord, he who created you, O Jacob, he who formed you, O Israel: 'Fear not, for I have redeemed you; I have called you by name, you are mine. When you pass through the waters I will be with you; and through the rivers, they shall not overwhelm you; when you walk through the fire you shall not be burned, and the flame shall not consume you. For I am the Lord your God, the Holy One of Israel, your Savior' " (Isa. 43:1–3, *RSV*).

**Notes**

1. Arthur J. Snider, "25 Most Distressing Events in Your Life," *Science Digest,* May, 1971, pp. 68–72.
2. Clark Blackburn and Norman Lobsenz, *How to Stay Married* (New York: Cowles Books, 1968), p. 196.
3. Antoinette Bosco, "What Happens to Parents When a Child Dies?" *Marriage and Family Living,* August, 1978; quoting Harriet Schiff, *The Bereaved Parent* (New York: Crown Publishers, 1977).
4. Bosco.
5. Bosco.
6. Lloyd H. Ahlem, *How to Cope with Crisis, Conflicts and Change* (Glendale, CA: Regal Books, 1978), p. 16.
7. Ahlem, p. 45. Adapted from "Crisis/Transition Sequence" chart by Ralph G. Hirschowitz, *Levinson Letter* (Cambridge: The Levinson Institute, Inc., n.d.), p. 4.

## CHAPTER NINE

# DETERMINING WHO MAKES DECISIONS

All couples develop a style of making decisions. Some styles are effective; some are self-defeating. How you make decisions in your marriage determines whether this pillar is strong and supportive or is weak and contributing to an eventual deterioration of your marriage.

For many couples, decision-making is one of the most unenjoyable and even painful aspects of marriage. A couple who has never developed skills for competent decision-making suffers the consequences. They are less effective in coping with problem situations than couples who have developed mutually agreeable decision-making methods. They experience frustration, anger, and stress. They feel unloved and end up being more dependent on others.

## WHAT DO YOU THINK?

1. Who makes most of the decisions, you or your spouse? Why? How was this arrangement reached?

2. What guidelines have you developed to distinguish between a "minor" and a "major" decision?

3. What course of action do you follow when you disagree on a decision? Who casts the deciding vote and why?

4. How have you decided which of the household chores each of you performs? Are you satisfied with the present distribution of household tasks?

5. Do you make any decisions without consulting your spouse? Which ones? How was this decided?

6. Do you make decisions that you want to make, or do you feel forced to decide in areas where you are uncomfortable? Which areas?

7. When are you most dominant in your marriage? When is your mate most dominant?

8. Do you feel that the Scriptures give any guidelines concerning which decisions to make? If so, what do the Scriptures say?

In the book *The Mirages of Marriage,* Don Jackson and Richard Lederer state that the failure of couples to identify, determine, and mutually assign areas of competence and responsibility, and determine who is in charge of what, is among the most destructive omissions in marriage.[1]

Certain tasks may appear quite clear-cut; many others are not. One myth that has been perpetuated over the years is the husband *must* be in charge of certain areas and the wife *must* be in charge of others. It's like saying certain tasks are male and certain tasks are female. This thinking keeps many couples from being able to use their unique talents and gifts adequately to enrich their marriage. It is very difficult for many evangelical Christians, to break away from this attitude.

If a person's temperaments, abilities, and training are not suited to an established cultural role, he may become frustrated and question his abilities. He may also find devious means to avoid the responsibility and increasing conflict in his marriage. His spouse may question his abilities too.

Even though we may not want or be able to fulfill the established cultural roles, our relationship requires order and an assignment of roles. Proverbs tells us:

"The plans of the heart belong to man, but the answer of the tongue is from the Lord" (16:1, *NASB*). "Commit your works to the Lord, and your plans will be established" (16:3, *NASB*). "The plans of the diligent lead surely to advantage, but everyone who is hasty comes surely to poverty" (21:5, *NASB*). This does not mean that role assignments and guidelines are locked into the marriage forever. They must be open to frequent revision.

One of the common complaints about establishing a marriage with a system of rules is that it is too rigid and unromantic. This system is thought to thwart the leading of the Holy Spirit in the relationship. Quite the contrary. Couples who overtly resist evaluating their marriage, setting goals, and determining the area of decision-making and roles are usually threatened because they feel insecure and inadequate. They also may not have developed a life-style of self-discipline. They may have to make some changes.

When a couple has guidelines for making decisions, their behaviors are predictable. Predictability develops trust in their relationship, which in turn allows freedom to develop exceptions to the rules when necessary. Assigning both authority and responsibilities creates flexibility in the relationship and thereby allows the couple to relax and give themselves to the tasks of enhancing their marriage and glorifying Christ.

What kind of trust do you want to develop as a couple? It is possible to develop negative trust as well as positive trust. If a spouse frequently does not live up to his promises or commitments, negative trust will develop. We can be predictable by not being trustworthy or dependable. This predictability, however, does not demonstrate love toward our partner. Spouses want the kind of predictability that creates positive trust.

There are at least three basic decision-making patterns. One is the *stepwise* pattern, in which the decision is made according to a specified order. For example, a couple could agree to work on a problem, select one part to discuss, suggest possible solutions, and so on. All of the steps do not necessarily need to occur at the same time, but the process, once begun, is carried out in steps.

A second approach is the *non-stepwise* pattern. This simply means that all of the activities carried out in the process of making a decision do not occur in order. Certain portions of the process are omitted or even repeated.

A third type of decision-making is the *defaulted* pattern. In this pattern the decision is actually made for the other person and occurs as a result of outside events, decisions, or a lack of decisions on the part of the partner.

1. As you reflect upon the past year, what are six decisions that were made by you and/or your spouse?

(1)

(2)

(3)

(4)

(5)

(6)

2. Now go back over your list and indicate how each decision was made. Was it made by the stepwise method, non-stepwise, or default?

3. What is the typical style of decision-making in your marriage?

4. How do you feel about this approach?

---

Decision issues are not all the same. It is important to determine which *type* of decision issues are involved. The decision issues that occur regularly are labeled *recurring* issues. They can involve many different areas and often recur because of inadequate discussion and planning. Some of these might involve how much money to spend on clothing and food, how often to have the car serviced, use of time for recreation, etc.

*Nonrecurring* issues are those that come only occasionally or once in a lifetime. They could involve where to live, changing jobs, a child's college education, and aging parents.

A *nonconjoint* issue is one in which both spouses are not

needed to make a decision. There are several forms or sub-types of nonconjoint issues. One is the decision in which the outcome affects only one of the spouses—what to eat for lunch, what to wear, etc.

Another subtype is the "factual" solution, where the outside evidence of facts actually decides the outcome for you. For example, if you want to purchase a new house, you may evaluate cost, interest, present savings, and income. You may then discover that purchasing the house is just not possible for you at this time; your decision has been made for you. It is your decision, but it is based on the input of other persons or situations.

A last subtype of a nonconjoint issue requires expert opinion. This kind of decision-making usually involves medical, religious, technical, or legal matters.

Perhaps you have never thought of the details of marital and family decisions like this. Many couples keep going on and on without any serious reflection about the types or styles of decisions, but close consideration may truly enhance and improve the relationship.

When we are making decisions, we encounter roadblocks. One roadblock is disagreeing on goals. When you disagree on goals, reaching a decision is difficult. Often couples don't know that their goals are different because they haven't talked about them!

Decisions tend to be poor when you try to solve too many problems at once. You may be eyeing one decision while still trying to make another. You may tend to insert elements from the second problem into the first, which only leads to confusion.

Decisions tend to be poor also when selfishness plays a major role. If I want my way and I'm determined to get it, I probably won't hear you. This approach can lead to retaliation. The application of Proverbs 18:13 and James 1:19 is not in effect here. "He who gives an answer before he hears, it is folly and shame to him" (Prov. 18:13, *NASB*). "Know this, my beloved brethren. Let every man be quick to hear, slow to speak, slow to anger" (Jas. 1:19, *RSV*).

Another problem in decision-making occurs when one or the other, or both, places more trust in the advice and opinions of others than in his spouse. If we feel that the outside advice we received was good and share it with our spouse, how do we respond if he doesn't accept our recommendations? From time to time, outside advice is helpful, but both spouses need to evaluate this information. When we seek outside advice, are we looking for an objective opinion or one that supports our viewpoint?

Deciding the opinion of our spouse and causing him to eventually question his opinions creates stress in decision-making. An "I told you so" attitude about decisions soon weakens the other's confidence in himself. Some decisions may turn out to be poor choices, but the responsibility for such should be mutual. Blaming or showing a superior attitude only weakens a relationship.

Who is the decision-maker in your marriage? Perhaps one person has been cast into the role of decision-maker. This is the expedient approach, and it may be functional; but reaching the decision appears to be more important than making the decision as a couple. This approach eliminates one person from the decision-making process, retarding his/her growth as well as their growth as a couple. One-party decisions may be faster, but do they help the development of the relationship? One-party decisions place the burden of certain areas of the marriage on just one person. If things go wrong, you may have to answer to the other person.

### WHAT DO YOU THINK?

Here is a decision-making guide to help you determine how much influence you have in the decision-making process. Follow the instructions.

Describe the decision-making process of your marriage by indicating the percentage of influence you have, and the percentage your spouse has, for each issue. The total for each decision must be 100 percent. (Those who write 50:50 too many times will be considered dishonest.)

| | Percentage of My Vote | Percentage of My Spouse's Vote | Who I feel is more qualified to contribute to this decision. (Write your initial or your spouse's.) |
|---|---|---|---|
| New car | | | |
| Home | | | |
| Furniture | | | |
| Your wardrobe | | | |
| Spouse's wardrobe | | | |
| Vacation spots | | | |
| Decor for the home | | | |
| Mutual friends | | | |
| Entertainment | | | |
| Church | | | |
| Child-rearing practices | | | |
| TV shows | | | |
| Home menu | | | |
| Number of children | | | |
| Where you live | | | |
| Husband's vocation | | | |
| Wife's vocation | | | |
| How money is spent | | | |
| How often to have sex | | | |
| Where to have sex | | | |
| Mealtimes | | | |
| Landscaping | | | |
| Various household tasks | | | |

It is commonly assumed that when a marriage contains a dominant spouse and a submissive spouse, the dominant one is the controlling one—in other words, the decision-maker. But in reality, the dominant one could be ineffective, because the submissive one probably controls the relationship through passive resistance, such as withdrawing, silence, and refusing to give an opinion.

Let's consider another factor about decision-making. Which of you makes the decisions more quickly? What effect does this have? In any relationship it is normal for one to be quicker and more decisive. This doesn't mean that the faster person is any more intelligent than the slower person.

The quicker spouse inserts his thoughts, his plan, his procedures into the discussion first and has a strong influence. He has the advantage, and thus the slower person tends to become even slower. He can't keep pace or catch up.

"In a marriage relationship it is usual for one to be quicker and more decisive than the other, and in the majority of cases the quicker decision-maker is at an advantage and his direction is usually adopted. The effect that this has on the slower person is that he tends to become slower and eventually give up. Why try? Thus he usually saves his response or reaction until the decision is made and then either shares approval or objections without having shared his thinking or reasoning on the matter."[2]

Father Chuck Gallagher suggests: "We can influence the other person to make a decision by our rate of speed. For example, a fast person may come up with one solution after another and force the other person to take one or another of what is offered. The slower one may initially turn down all of them, but after a while feels that he has been too negative by saying no, no, no. So he says yes just because so many solutions are presented.

"On the other hand, a slow person can also exert pressure. He can give the impression that he is reliable, thoughtful, and more to be trusted in making decisions, thus implying that the other person is rash or inexact. The ponderous person can be so slow-moving—examining every little detail—that he frustrates the other party to pieces.

"A slow person can even put the blame on the partner when things go wrong and say, 'Because you rushed so, you made me come to a decision when I wasn't ready for it—I didn't have time to think it through.'

"It is better that there be a commitment by both spouses to get involved in the overall decision-making process. We have to develop a 'couple-pace' of making decisions rather than maintaining our individual paces. The slow person can learn to go a bit faster, and the faster one can learn to slow down. The point is to formulate our decisions together.

"Of course, we may differ in other ways in our decision-making. One of us may be sharp, clear, definitive and decisive. The other one might be cautious, gentle, investigative, option-oriented. Each of these qualities is good and has definite advantages. But if we maintain our individual qualities and don't mesh ours with our spouse's, everything imaginable can occur."[3]

Where do we go from here in our decision-making? Consider these questions as a plan for evaluation and implementation:

*If you and your spouse could show a film of your parents' marital style, would you see your marriage reflected there?* Are the responsibilities and control in the marriage divided on the basis of traditional role expectations or upon what your own parents did? Traditional role structures are rigid in most cases, but some find definite security within the system. However, when one partner begins to ask, "Why do we do it this way?" or when children grow up and leave, problems may emerge. When a couple's life-style changes, the process of decision-making and role responsibilities change. Should the husband be the one to wash the car, mow the lawn, fix the roof? Should the wife be the one to cook, do the housework, and care for the children? There may be more creative ways of functioning than following the traditional roles.

*Is the responsibility for making decisions based on your abilities and giftedness?* Does the control shift back and forth from one to another? If so, you probably have a very efficient marriage in which each partner can be creative and grow as an individual.

Louis and Colleen Evans suggest cultivating spiritual gifts into the arena of roles and decision-making: "One of the first steps in putting gifts of the Spirit to work in a marriage is to *believe* in such a thesis and to enter into the process of becoming aware, sensitive, and on the lookout for indications of your own and others' gifts.

"Not all men are gifted in financial management; sometimes the wives are. In many mature and happy Christian homes we have seen the wife take the initiative in financial matters. True, there was always discussion about the decisions, and in the great majority of the circumstances, there was agreement. But in each, there was a quiet acceptance of her gift and an acquiescence to her counsel even though the 'man was the head of the house.'

"Some men are not gifted in teaching; to require them to be the spiritual teacher as 'head of the family' would be to put a heavy burden on their backs as well as create an atmosphere of awkwardness in the process, which repels rather than attracts the student. That does not mean a man might not 'teach' in his own style of actions and responses to life's situations.

"If the wife's gift is discovered to be something that takes her outside the home, then she and her husband need to consider the place of children in their marriage. If they feel children are right for them, then they ought to set aside the time to do the job right without feeling 'hemmed in' or becoming the victims of 'cabin fever.' The mature woman will not feel pushed out of shape or frustrated in the role of childbearing; she will be able to give herself to this process with joy and delight, for this is a phase of her life. If she cannot raise

126

children in this attitude, then for God's sake and the child's sake she shouldn't have children; no one wants to feel unwanted or that he or she is an inconvenience. But so many, not wanting to 'make the sacrifice,' are yet pressured by the 'standard role' and have children, resisting all the way."[4]

In this relationship it is important that each person be aware of what the other is thinking and the direction in which he is growing, so they can discuss issues knowledgeably. One caution, however, if you have specific areas of responsibility and decision-making for each of you, be sure to be as informed as possible concerning the other areas. Some couples have developed an isolation from each other because they divided their responsibilities to an extreme and failed to share them. Direct involvement and communication will eliminate this potential problem.

*Does one spouse fail to assume responsibility for making decisions, thus forcing the other to make the decision?* Some couples do not make decisions but allow them to happen. This has been called decision by default. Usually the one who is affected least by the decision allows the other to make it. This approach is not always satisfactory. As long as one partner takes the abdicated responsibility, he reinforces the apathy of the other. It might be best not to take the responsibility so readily but to discuss the matter fully.

Too many husbands turn the responsibility for child-rearing decisions over to their wives, but the Scriptures indicate that the father is to be involved with the child. Note the following verses describing the father's task:

To chasten—Proverbs 19:18

To correct—Proverbs 22:15; 23:13

To teach—Deuteronomy 6:7; 11:18–21; Proverbs 1:8; 4:1–4

To nurture—Ephesians 6:4

Not to provoke to anger—Colossians 3:21

To provide for—1 Timothy 5:8; 2 Corinthians 12:14

To encourage—1 Thessalonians 2:11
To command—Genesis 18:19
To guide—Jeremiah 3:4
To discipline—Proverbs 3:12; Hebrews 12:5–7

*Do you discuss together your methods for making decisions?* What is the reason for this?

Sit down together during a time when no major decision must be made and work out the process that you will follow. List three suggestions that you could offer to your spouse to help in the decision-making process.

Many couples develop a special, agreed-upon decision time, during which issues can be discussed, one at a time, with no interruptions. Try to carry the decision issue to the point of conclusion.

*Is your plan for decision-making successful?* If you and your spouse are using a set method of making decisions and it is not working well, experiment with another method. Different approaches need to be developed.

*Have you ever asked your spouse if he has difficulty making decisions?* Is it easy for him? Which areas are easy and which are difficult? Does he know whether it is difficult for you or easy for you? You cannot always judge by his outward behavior. He may be experiencing some inner conflict and may welcome input from you.

*Have you agreed to make decisions in certain areas on your own without interference from your spouse?* Many couples have numerous areas in which one is responsible for making decisions on his own. Some couples put a dollar limit on household or hobby items and do not have to consult the other unless the price exceeds the limit. One man stated in one of our marriage enrichment seminars that in the last 10 years he had not purchased one new item of clothing for himself. His wife buys everything, and he is very satisfied with this arrangement. He hates to shop, and he trusts her judgment. One couple stated that when they purchase a car that she will drive, she is primarily responsible for the choice, and when it is for him, he has more to say.

*What are some of the major decisions that each of you makes?* What are the minor ones? Who decides which are minor and which are major? How do you feel about these decisions? Is there an area in which you would like some assistance from your spouse or one in which you would like a greater voice? Some couples have written job division lists and then considered who has the time, ability, and expertise to get each job done. They consider who is more concerned with each area and who enjoys the task the most.[5]

"[It is] essential to realize that the spouse who *makes* the decisions is not necessarily the spouse who *controls* them. The key question ultimately is, 'Who *decides* who decides?'

"Husbands or wives often 'delegate' decision areas to their partners so that while the actual decision is made by one, there is no doubt that the other holds the power. As we have pointed out, sometimes the 'weaker' partner may actually have his or her mate jumping through hoops. A 'helpless' husband may ask his wife to lay out his clothing every morning so that his socks, shoes, tie, shirt, and suit will coordinate. *She decides* what he will wear, but *he has decided* that she is to be his 'valet.' A 'depressed' wife may have everyone in the household catering to her 'bad' days. Many books and articles have been written telling wives how to fool husbands into believing they are 'lords and masters' by appearing to defer to them on the surface. This game playing backfires in the long run. Finding the patterns you use to make decisions, altering them to suit your needs, and having a variety of decision-making methods to use for different circumstances are the realistic and effective techniques that make a marriage function well."[6]

*Do our thoughts and decisions reflect our relationship with the Lord?* The one person most often left out of the decision-making process is Jesus Christ. The lordship of

Christ means His direction should be involved in our decisions. Colossians 3:17 states: "And whatever you do in word or deed, do all in the name of the Lord Jesus, giving thanks through Him to God the Father" (*NASB*).

We read in Ephesians 4:23 that we are to "be renewed in the spirit of your mind." Renewing the spirit of our mind means that which gives the mind the direction and contents of its thoughts. This passage speaks of God's Spirit influencing man's mental attitude. This should also include our reasons and motivations for our decisions.

One of the major questions usually asked has to do with the impasse. When each person is committed to his own point of view or belief, further negotiation seems unlikely to produce any change.

James Jauncey, in his book *Magic in Marriage,* points out that the Christian husband and wife have specific help for everyday problems, not only from the guidelines in the Scriptures, but also in the daily presence of the Holy Spirit. Jauncey says:

"God through His Holy Spirit seeks our best welfare and happiness. He seldom does this by a supernatural act. Instead, He seeks to permeate our thinking until our judgments are His.

"In marriage He has two people to work through. The husband's authority does not carry infallibility with it. Since the two have become 'one flesh' the guidance has to come through both. This means that except in cases of emergency, decisions affecting the whole family should not be put into effect until they are unanimous."[7]

## WHAT'S YOUR PLAN?

1. List 12 areas of decision-making in your marriage.

(1)                              (3)

(2)                              (4)

| (5) | (9) |
|-----|-----|
| (6) | (10) |
| (7) | (11) |
| (8) | (12) |

Now indicate which of these are major decision areas and which are minor.

2. List 12 areas of responsibility in your marriage.

| (1) | (7) |
|-----|-----|
| (2) | (8) |
| (3) | (9) |
| (4) | (10) |
| (5) | (11) |
| (6) | (12) |

Who has time to do these?


Who likes to do them?


Who has the greatest ability to do them?


Who is most concerned about their getting done?


Who actually completes each task?

3. Look at the time sequence listed below. Indicate the major decisions you will need to make during the time periods indicated. These decisions may concern your personal life, vocation, children, other family members, vacations, etc.

Within the next 5 years:

Within the next 10 years:

Within the next 15 years:

Within the next 20 years:

Within the next 30 years:

Which of you will have the most to contribute concerning each decision? Why? In what way will the Word of God help you in these decisions?

## Notes

1. Don Jackson and Richard Lederer, *The Mirages of Marriage* (New York: W.W. Norton & Co., 1968), pp. 248, 249.
2. H. Norman Wright, *The Family that Listens* (Wheaton, IL: Scripture Press, 1978), pp. 32, 33.
3. Chuck Gallagher, *Love Is a Couple* (New York: Sadlier Publishers, 1976), pp. 76, 77.
4. Louis Evans, Jr., and Colleen Evans, "Gifts of the Spirit in Marriage," as quoted in Gary Collins, ed., *Make More of Your Marriage* (Waco, TX: Word Books, 1976), pp. 38, 39.
5. Adapted from Marcia Laswell and Norman M. Lobsenz, *No Fault Marriage: The New Technique of Self-Counseling and What It Can Help You Do* (Garden City, NY: Doubleday & Co., 1976).
6. Laswell and Lobsenz, p. 221.
7. James Jauncey, *Magic in Marriage* (Waco, TX: Word Books, 1968), pp. 126, 127.

## CHAPTER TEN

# WHAT CAUSES CONFLICTS AND QUARRELS?

"What causes conflicts and quarrels among you? Do they not spring from the aggressiveness of your bodily desires? You want something which you cannot have, and so you are bent on murder; you are envious, and cannot attain your ambition, and so you quarrel and fight. You do not get what you want, because you do not pray for it. Or, if you do, your requests are not granted because you pray from wrong motives" (Jas. 4:1–3, *NEB*).

These strong words were written to Christians many years ago, yet they are words that are applicable today for many married couples. Many marriages are characterized by strife and bickering rather than peace and harmony. Couples who have developed harmony are not those who are identical in thinking, behavior, and attitudes—they are not carbon copies of each other. They are the couples who have learned to take their differences through the process of acceptance, understanding and, eventually, complementation. Differing from another person is very natural and normal and adds an edge of excitement to a relationship.

Because each person is unique and because what each brings to the marriage is unique, conflict will emerge. In fact, there will be numerous conflicts throughout the life of the marriage. This is not bad; this is normal. How you respond to the conflicts and deal with them is the real issue.

Let's define conflict. "Conflict, . . . to strike together. 1. a fight, clash, contention. 2. sharp disagreement or opposition, as of interests, ideas, etc., mutual interference of incompatible forces or wills."[1] Many couples learn to avoid conflict. They attempt to ignore or bury differences. They fail to realize that when their differences are buried, they are buried alive and at some time will resurrect themselves.

One of the traditional ways couples learn to deal with conflict is to suppress it—try to forget it, sweep it under the rug, or shrug it off. This so-called nice way has been equated with being Christian. Burying conflicts, however, only builds resentments, which drain you of energy and color your entire perception of daily life.

Another way couples handle conflict is to express their feelings unreservedly. For some couples this approach resembles a war. Wave after wave of attack seems to mount, and the intensity increases. In time verbal garbage is thrown, computer memories are activated (and these would put an elephant's memory to shame), and total frustration is the end result. During this time each assumes the role of a skilled lawyer, eager not only to indict the other but to see him convicted (and in some cases hung!).

"So let us look more closely at marital conflict. Marriage is the coming together of two unique and different individuals in order to share life with each other. Their differences are quite unavoidable. They have lived separate lives for perhaps twenty to twenty-five years, during which each has developed a set of individual tastes, preferences, habits, likes and dislikes, values and standards. It is totally unreasonable to suppose that two people, just because they are married to each other, should always want to do the same thing in the same way at the same time.

"This doesn't happen even with identical twins. So the couple have differences of opinion and of choice, and these differences lead to disagreements. The couple may be quite willing to do the same thing in the same way, but at different

134

times; or to do the same thing at the same time, but in different ways. How do you solve this problem? Either they must
give up the idea altogether, and both feel frustrated and
blame each other; or one will have to give up his particular
wish and do it in the way, or at the time, the other wishes.
People in love are able to do a good deal of giving up and
giving in because love creates a generous mood. But sooner or
later a situation develops in which neither is willing to accom-
modate the other because patience is exhausted, or enough
ground has already been surrendered, or this time it is a
matter of principle. So they are deadlocked, and now we have
a conflict."[2]

Unresolved conflicts do not diminish but continue to grow
and grow. Notice the progression as indicated in this chart.[3]

| Difference of opinion | "Spat" | Confrontation |
| --- | --- | --- |
| Heated debate or argument | "Quarrel" | Division |
| Intense physical anger | "Fight" | Rejection |
| Hostility confirmed | "War" | Separation |

Differences and disagreements in marriage is the rule and not
the exception. Every couple at one time or another will be
angry and have arguments and complaints against each
other.

Conflict has been called *a positive sign of marital
growth*. Do you agree? Perhaps not, if conflict in your experience has been overly painful, unresolved, or buried. But some
areas of conflict are to be expected at the various stages in the
life cycle of a marriage. Marriages pass through stages of
development as people do. Think of the potential differences
or conflicts that can emerge when:
- the first child is born
- the second child is born
- a spouse has to work 12 hours a day while the other is home
  with three preschoolers

- a child has an accident while under the supervision of one of the parents, and the insurance does not cover the $600 medical bill
- the last child leaves home
- retirement comes and both are now at home

Or think of some of these differences between the couple. Are they potential for conflict?

- one is a bottom-of-the-toothpaste-tube squeezer, and the other squeezes from the top
- one wants the toilet paper rolled from the top of the roll, and the other wants it rolled from the bottom
- one's body temperature cries for the thermostat to be set at 78 degrees, and the other is constantly flinging open the windows
- when they speak, one gives an entire novel-length story, and the other gives a two-line news summary
- one is a night person and the other a morning person
- one wants the room absolutely dark for sleeping, and the other wants a light on
- one feels that making love belongs only in the bedroom in the dark and under the covers, but the other likes variety and is quite inventive
- one tosses and hangs the clothes wherever he feels led, and the other has the clothes color-coded and on the hangers a half-inch apart
- one likes to arrive 15 minutes late and the other 15 minutes early

**WHAT DO YOU THINK?**

1. List eight minor or subtle differences between the ways you and your spouse think, believe, and do things.

2. Now go back over your list and check those which have created conflict in your marriage.

3. Which of these differences are really important and significant?

4. What major conflicts have you experienced in your marriage?

---

In the chart earlier in this chapter the word *quarrel* was indicated. Many couples state that what pains them most about conflict is the constant quarreling that occurs. Other couples say they avoid conflict, if at all possible, because of the biblical teaching concerning quarreling. What does the Bible say about conflict? What does it say about quarrels? Are quarreling and conflict synonymous? Not really. Many conflicts are handled and resolved without quarreling.

A quarrel has been defined as verbal strife in which angry emotions are in control and the couple does not deal with the issue but instead attacks the other person. This behavior creates strain in their relationship. The Scriptures tell us not to be involved in quarrels: "It is an honor for a man to cease from strife and keep aloof from it, but every fool will be quarreling" (Prov. 20:3, *AMP*). "As coals are to hot embers, and wood to fire, so is a quarrelsome man to inflame strife" (Prov. 26:21, *AMP*). "Let all bitterness and indignation and wrath (passion, rage, bad temper) and resentment (anger, animosity) and quarreling (brawling, clamor, contention) and slander . . . be banished from you" (Eph. 4:31, *AMP*).

Let's consider some beliefs and assumptions about conflict.

*Conflict is a natural phenomenon and is therefore inevitable.* Conflict arises in part because all of us perceive people and situations differently. These different perceptions allow for different opinions and choices which can cause conflict. And conflict is inevitable between people who care about each other and want to develop a deeper relationship. Dwight Small says:

"The most frequent conflicts husbands and wives experience are verbal. Verbal conflict in itself is not harmful; any damage it causes depends upon the maturity of the two people in conflict. Entirely different ends can be served by a verbal clash, and some of them are healthy and good. Conflict can open doors of communication as well as shut them. As a reality in marriage, conflict can be creatively managed for good; it is part of the growth process. Don't ever underestimate its positive possibilities!"[4]

"In Christian marriage, conflict—with its demand for confession, forgiveness, and reconciliation—is a means God employs to teach humility."[5]

*Conflict involves personal values and needs.* Every human being has some very basic needs. William Glasser suggests that the most basic are the need to love and be loved, and the need to feel worthwhile. Abraham Maslow describes a hierarchy of needs. Remember what they were? We strive to fulfill our physiological needs first, then our safety needs, our need for love and belongingness, need for esteem, and self-actualization needs. When you have a conflict, consider which of your needs are not being met.

*Conflicts usually emerge as a symptom.* When people find themselves in conflict they usually have some need that is unfulfilled. Resolving the conflict may not solve the problem. It is better to look below the symptom, discover what need the person is striving to fulfill, and resolve that rather than the symptom only.

*Most conflict is not dealt with openly because most people have not been taught effective ways of resolving conflict.* Many couples ignore minor conflicts to keep from rocking the boat. When a major conflict arises, people tend to avoid it because they have not learned how to deal with minor conflicts. They have not developed the necessary skills by solving minor problems.

Urban G. Wiese and Bernard R. Steinmetz say about conflict: "Disagreements are inevitable at many points in marriage and family living. Sometimes spouses become competitors as well as helpers and complements to one another. Rather than the isolation and alienation which accompanies conflict too often in the home, couples need to overcome the loneliness, to reduce the personal hurt, retaliation and recrimination. To accomplish this, differences must be brought out into the open so that good communication can be restored. Angry reactions are inevitable in a person's life, especially in the closeness and intimacy of family life, but the most important consideration is what one does with anger."[6]

*Conflict provides opportunity for growth in a relationship.* Conflict is like dynamite. It can be helpful if used in the right way but can also be destructive if used at the wrong time or in the wrong manner. Through conflict a person can share his differences with another individual. Facing conflict is also a way of testing one's own strength and resources. Each person in a conflict situation will bring one or more alternative choices to the discussion. These can be explored together, and each can learn from the other. When the conflict is resolved, there can be growth on the part of both individuals.

Again, Dr. Small states: "Disagreements come and they must be handled in one way or another. . . . We must also make the distinction that disagreements are one thing, behaving disagreeably is quite another."[7]

139

*Unresolved conflicts interfere with growth and satisfying relationships.* Barriers are erected when conflicts are not resolved. We tend to become defensive in order not to be hurt. A defensive reaction places a strain on any relationship.[8]

Jesus experienced conflict. He was in constant conflict with the religious leaders of Judea. They wanted to defeat Jesus. They wanted to win over Him. John 8:1–11 is an account of one of the conflicts between Jesus and the religious leaders. You are probably familiar with the story. Here is a paraphrase of the incident:

"Early next morning Jesus returned to the Temple and all the people there gathered around him as he began to teach. Then the scribes and the Pharisees brought in a woman caught in adultery. They stood her before Jesus and said, 'Teacher, this woman was caught in the very act and in the law, Moses said we are to stone such a woman to death. What do you say?' They did this as a trap to catch Jesus in some break with the Law, so they could charge him. . . . But Jesus responded, 'Let him among you who has never sinned throw the first stone at her. . . .' And when they heard what he said they went out one by one, leaving the woman standing there before Jesus. Then Jesus stood up and spoke to her. 'Where are they all? Has no one condemned you?' And she replied, 'No one, sir.' 'Neither do I condemn you,' said Jesus. 'Go home, and do not sin again.' "[9]

Jesus did not run or withdraw from this confrontation. Neither did He yield to their demands, nor did He compromise, but forced the scribes and Pharisees to consider an alternative—mercy for the woman.

## WHAT DO YOU THINK?

David Augsburger says: "Of the five options in conflict situations—(1) I win—you lose, (2) I want out, I'll withdraw, (3) I'll give in for good relations, (4) I'll meet you halfway, (5) I can care and confront—the last is the most effective, the most truly loving, the most growth-promoting for human relationships. But all five have their rightful place, their proper time for usage, their appropriate moment.''[10]

---

Using David Augsburger's description of dealing with conflict, tell which method you think Jesus used in each of the four following situations. Some of the passages are given in detail and some are paraphrased. If you need a description of the entire situation, read the passage from the Scriptures.

1. Healing on the Sabbath: "And He entered again into a synagogue; and a man was there with a withered hand. And they were watching Him to see if He would heal him on the Sabbath, in order that they might accuse Him. And He said to the man with the withered hand, 'Rise and come forward!' And He said to them, 'Is it lawful on the Sabbath to do good or to do harm, to save a life or to kill?' But they kept silent. And after looking around at them with anger, grieved at their hardness of heart, He said to the man, 'Stretch out your hand.' And he stretched it out, and his hand was restored" (Mark 3:1–5, *NASB*). How did Jesus handle this conflict?

2. The tradition of handwashing: "Jesus was approached by a group of Pharisees and lawyers from Jerusalem, with the question: 'Why do your disciples break the ancient tradition? They do not wash their hands before meals.' He answered them: 'And what of you? Why do you break God's commandment in the interest of your tradition? For God said, "Honour your father and mother," and "The man who curses his father or mother must suffer death." But you say, "If a man says to his father or mother, 'Anything of mine which might have been used for your benefit is set apart for God,' then he must not honour his father or his mother." You have made God's law null and void out of respect for your tradition. What hypocrisy! Isaiah was right when he prophesied about you: "This people pays me lip-service, but their heart is far from me; their worship of me is in vain, for they teach as doctrines

the commandments of men" ' " (Matt. 15:1–9, *NEB*; see also verses 10–20). How did Jesus handle this conflict?

3. Withdrawing to the wilderness: Neither His biblical reasoning nor the remarkable works that He did among the people convinced the religious leaders that Jesus was their long-awaited Messiah-Christ. Instead they sought to kill Him for this blasphemous claim. Later Jesus deliberately exposed Himself to their conspiracies. But He preferred to choose His own time to go up to them in Jerusalem. So until He was ready for that confrontation, He took His disciples and withdrew into the wilderness. "Accordingly Jesus no longer went about publicly in Judaea, but left that region for the country bordering on the desert, and came to a town called Ephraim, where he stayed with his disciples" (setting: John 11:54, *NEB;* see vv. 45–57). How did Jesus handle this conflict?

4. Facing the temple money changers: When Jesus did come to Jerusalem, His actions against the sacrifice-sellers and money changers jolted everyone. "And he . . . began to drive out those who sold and those who bought in the temple . . . and said to them, 'Is it not written, "My house shall be called a house of prayer for all nations"? But you have made it a den of robbers' " (Mark 11:15–17, *RSV*; see vv. 11–19). How did Jesus handle this conflict?[11]

## WHAT'S YOUR PLAN?

1. If you could improve the manner in which you and your spouse handle conflicts, what would you change?

2. What is one conflict area that you would like to see resolved at the present time and one that you would be willing to discuss with your spouse this week?

142

## Notes

1. James G.T. Fairfield, *When You Don't Agree* (Scottdale, PA: Herald Press, 1977), p. 18.
2. David and Vera Mace, *We Can Have Better Marriages if We Really Want Them* (Nashville: Abingdon Press, 1974), pp. 88–90.
3. Fairfield, p. 19.
4. Dwight Small, *After You've Said I Do* (Old Tappan, NJ: Fleming H. Revell, 1968), p. 137.
5. Small, p. 130.
6. Urban G. Wiese and Bernard R. Steinmetz, *Everything You Need to Know to Stay Married and Like It* (Grand Rapids: Zondervan, 1972), p. 45.
7. Small, p. 139.
8. Section on conflict adapted from H. Norman Wright, *Communication and Conflict Resolution in Marriage* (Elgin, IL: David C. Cook, 1977), p. 9.
9. Fairfield, p. 9.
10. David Augsburger, *Caring Enough to Confront* (Glendale, CA: Regal Books, 1973), p. 11.
11. Settings adapted from Fairfield, pp. 39, 40.

## CHAPTER ELEVEN

# DEALING WITH MARITAL CONFLICT

All of us, upon entering marriage, develop a style of dealing with conflict. We might assume that our spouse will handle conflict in a similar manner, but there are many ways of handling conflict. These differences are at the heart of much of the conflict.

David and Vera Mace suggest that the conflict process looks like Diagram 15.

DIAGRAM 15

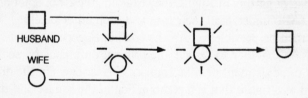

DIFFERENCES ▶ DISAGREEMENT ▶ CONFLICT ▶ RESOLUTION

"First we see the difference between husband and wife, illustrated by different shapes—a square and a circle. Next we see the difference in their wishes brought close together as a result of their desire for mutual involvement, which leads to

145

a disagreement—each is asking the other to yield.

"If they continue to confront each other in a state of disagreement, frustration is stirred in both and a state of emotional heat develops. This is conflict. They are moving into a clash of wills, a quarrel, a fight.

"What they do next is critical. If they can't tolerate conflict, they will disengage and go back to where they started. The difference remains unresolved. The disagreement is recognized, but avoided in future, and the feelings of frustration suppressed. The attempt to become more deeply involved with each other, in that particular area of their relationship, is abandoned."[1]

It is interesting to note that it is not the longer couples are married the more they have to talk about. It is more accurate to say that the longer couples are married the more they learn what *not* to talk about. And in doing this they erect barricades, which soon are reconstructed into walls, and live with certain areas of isolation between them. But there is another way of approaching conflict, which the Maces described:

"But suppose now that they recognize conflict as a friend in disguise and let their emotions heat up. And suppose that, instead of getting in a fight, they examine these hot emotions and try to understand their own and each other's feelings. It will then be possible to turn the conflict to good account by working together to resolve the original difference by some kind of adjustment or compromise. This is shown in the diagram as a figure that is a combination of the square and the circle."[2]

There are five basic ways of dealing with marital conflict:

*The first way is to withdraw.* If you have a tendency to see conflict as a hopeless inevitability and one which you can do little to control, then you may not even bother trying. You may withdraw physically by removing yourself from the room or environment, or you may withdraw psychologically by not speaking, ignoring, or insulating yourself so much that what is said or suggested has no penetrating power. There are many who use the backing-off approach to protect themselves.

*Winning is another alternative.* If your self-concept is threatened or if you feel strongly that you must look after your own interests, then this method may be your choice. If you have a position of authority and it becomes threatened, winning is a counterattack. No matter what the cost, winning is the goal.

People employ many different tactics in order to win. Since married couples are so well aware of each other's areas of vulnerability and hurt they often use these areas to coerce the other person into giving in to their own demands. "Winners" may attack self-esteem or pride in order to win. They may store up grudges and use them at the appropriate time in order to take care of a conflict. They may cash in old emotions and hurts at an opportune moment. The stockpiling approach is another form of revenge and certainly does not reflect a Christian's demonstration of forgiveness.

If winning is your style, answer the following questions:

1. Is winning necessary to build or maintain your self-esteem or to maintain a strong picture of yourself? People need strong self-esteem in order to find satisfaction in life and in their marriage. But what is the foundation upon which this is built? If one is insecure or doubtful, he often creates a false image to fool others and in the process confuses himself. To defer to another, to give in, or to lose a debate or argument is a strong threat to the person's feelings about himself, and thus he fights so that this will not happen. The authoritarian person is not usually as secure as the image he portrays. Deferring to another is a sign of a weakening of his position.

2. Is winning necessary because you confuse wants with needs? The spouse who feels he needs something may be more demanding about getting it than if he just wants something. Do you really distinguish between needs and wants? You may see something as a *need* in your life, but your partner may see

it as a *want*. How do you know if something truly is a need?

*A third approach to handling conflict is yielding*. We often see yield signs on the highway; they are placed there for our own protection. If we yield in a conflict, we also protect ourselves. We do not want to risk a confrontation, so we give in to get along with our partner.

We all use this approach from time to time, but is yielding a regular pattern for you? Consistent yielding may create feelings of martyrdom or eventually may create guilt in our partner. We even find some individuals who need to "lose" in a marital conflict. This approach is a face-saving way of doing that. By yielding, you give the appearance that you are in control and are the one behaving in the "most Christian" way.

We learn to suppress or repress our anger and pile it up instead of doing what Nehemiah did when he heard of the mistreatment of the poor people. "I [Nehemiah] was very angry when I heard their cry and these words. I thought it over, then rebuked the nobles and officials" (Neh. 5:6, 7, *AMP*). Some people gain as much from defeat as others do from winning.

*Another method of dealing with conflict is compromising or giving a little to get a little*. You have discovered that it is important to back off on some of your ideas or demands in order to help the other person give a little. You don't want to win all the time, nor do you want the other person to win all the time. This approach involves concessions on both sides and has been called the "horse trading" technique.

*A fifth method is called resolve*. In this style of dealing with conflicts, a situation, attitude, or behavior is changed by open and direct communication. The couple is willing to spend sufficient time working on the difference so that even though some of their original wants and ideas have changed, they are very satisfied with the solution they have arrived at.

Diagram 16 shows a way of diagramming the five styles of handling conflict.

DIAGRAM 16

## FIVE CONFLICT STYLES

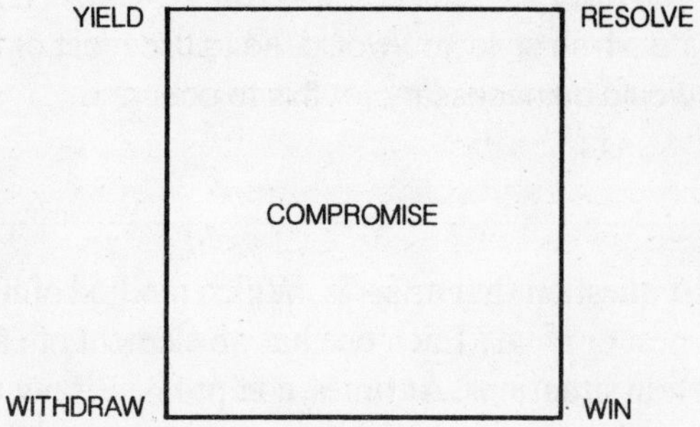

| | | |
|---|---|---|
| YIELD | | RESOLVE |
| | COMPROMISE | |
| WITHDRAW | | WIN |

## WHAT DO YOU THINK?

1. Turn to chapter 10 to the section that discussed Jesus' style of handling conflict. In each passage shared, decide which method was used.

2. Realizing that we may employ more than one method of handling conflict and may even use all five of the methods from time to time, indicate which style you use most of the time.

3. How does your style of reacting to conflict affect your marital relationship? How do you feel about it?

4. Which style does your spouse use most of the time?

5. Which style would your spouse say that you use most of the time?

6. Indicate which style you would like to use most of the time and what would be necessary for this to occur.

---

The next question that arises is, Which method of handling conflict is best or ideal? Each one has an element of effectiveness in certain situations. At times, compromise is not the best whereas winning may be. Yielding on certain occasions can be a true and pure act of love and concern. But the ideal style that we work toward is that of resolving conflicts.

Let's look at our diagram once again. (Diagram 17.)

DIAGRAM 17

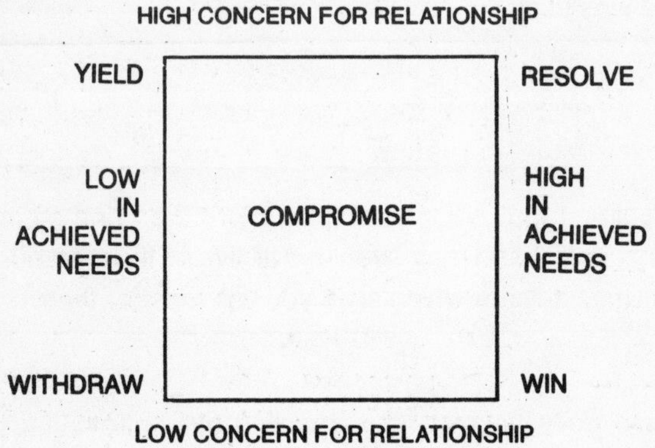

HIGH CONCERN FOR RELATIONSHIP

| YIELD | | RESOLVE |
|---|---|---|
| LOW IN ACHIEVED NEEDS | COMPROMISE | HIGH IN ACHIEVED NEEDS |
| WITHDRAW | | WIN |

LOW CONCERN FOR RELATIONSHIP

You will notice that some new descriptive words have been added this time. When a person uses *withdrawal* as his normal pattern of handling conflict, the relationship suffers and it is difficult to see needs being fulfilled. This is the least helpful style of handling conflicts. The relationship is hindered from growing and developing.

If this is your style, consider the reasons for this. It is not a demonstration of biblical submission or meekness. This method is often employed out of fear—fear of the other person or of one's own abilities.

*Winning* achieves the individual's goal but at the same time sacrifices the relationship. A person might win the battle but lose the war. In a marriage, personal relationships are more important than the goal, and winning can be a hollow victory.

*Yielding* has a higher value because it appears to build the relationship, but personal goals or needs are sacrificed in yielding, which can breed resentment. Yielding may not build the relationship as much as some believe, because if the relationship were that important, a person would be willing to share, confront, and become assertive. What can be accomplished through resolution will build the relationship even more and shows a greater concern for the relationship than do other methods.

*Compromising* is an attempt to work out the relationship and the achievement of some needs. The bargaining involved may mean that some values are compromised. You may find that you are not very satisfied with the end result, but it is better than nothing. This could actually threaten the relationship. There may be a feeling of uneasiness following the settlement.

*Resolving* conflict is the ideal toward which couples are encouraged to work. The relationship is strengthened when conflicts are resolved and needs are met on both sides. It takes longer and involves listening and acceptance.

"A Christian response to disagreements includes a willingness to be patient in working out a solution.

"The willingness to exchange information, feelings, and ideas with one another leads to mutual understanding. Our first idea about a problem will not always be the same as our later understandings of it. As new ideas are expressed and the discussion develops, the issues may change."[3]

You may have changed in the process, but you are glad for the change. It is positive and beneficial. And change is possible and necessary! Because Jesus Christ is present in our life, we can give up our fears and insecurities. We can have a new boldness and courage to confront the issues of life and, in a loving manner, others around us. Some people feel that it is impossible for them to change. But the Word of God says, "I can do all things through Christ which strengtheneth me" (Phil. 4:13, *KJV*).

## WHAT DO YOU THINK?

1. Looking at the five styles of handling conflict, describe a situation in which each style would be acceptable and alright to use.

STYLE          SITUATION

Withdraw

Win

Yield

Compromise

Resolving

2. Can you think of any biblical teaching that would assist you?

3. If resolving were to be your usual method of dealing with conflict, what changes would you need to make in order to make this a reality?

4. What changes would your spouse need to make to help in this process?

---

You may have decided that you would like to have *resolve* as your style but are wondering what to do to bring that about. Here is a suggested format to help move you to the style of resolve rather than to the other four. These suggestions will work if you spend time, make the effort, and persevere. Since conflict relates to the process of communication, and since it is impossible to separate the two, many of these suggestions are basic principles of communication. These principles are not necessarily listed in order of importance.

*Speak directly and personally to the other person.* Don't assume that the other person knows what you are thinking or feeling. If anything, assume that he knows very little and that this is his first time to deal with the issue. "In the end, people appreciate frankness more than flattery" (Prov. 28:23, *TLB*).

*Be honest in your statements and questions.* Ephesians 4:15 and 25 are important to practice both in making statements and in asking questions. When you ask a question, does the other person have the freedom to share his honest response? Even if you disagree with his response? If you feel that your partner has a double message behind his question or has an ulterior motive, respond only to the question at its face value. Don't get caught up in mind reading or second guessing.

*Make statements out of your questions.* Too often in a conflict one or the other feels as if he is in an inquisition.

*Focus on your desired expectations or positive changes* rather than on faults or defects or what you hope to avoid. This helps each of you become aware of what is gratifying and helpful to the other. Believe it or not, psychologically it is easier to begin new behaviors than to terminate old behaviors. Don't apologize for your feelings or your needs. "Therefore encourage (admonish, exhort) one another and edify— strengthen and build up—one another, just as you are doing" (1 Thess. 5:11, *AMP*).

When you are sharing what you want in a conflict, *share your request in a statement of preference* rather than a statement of necessity.

When you feel unloved by your partner, *initiate loving behavior toward your spouse*. Often when we feel that others do not love us, we may believe that we are not worth loving. If you begin to perform loving acts your spouse might act more loving toward you, but if not, that's all right. Your act of love can fulfill some of your own needs and is also a demonstration of Christ's love toward another person. Remember that real marital love is an unconditional commitment to an imperfect person.

*Make "I" statements rather than "you" statements* and share your *present* feelings rather than past thoughts or feelings.[4] The Minnesota Couples Communication Program has suggested a healthy model for expressing oneself in this way. The model includes four "Skills for Expressing Self-Awareness": speaking for self rather than for others; documenting with descriptive behavioral data; making feeling statements (speaking about oneself); making intention statements (speaking about oneself).

1. *Speaking for self:*

Husband: "I'd like to go out tonight."

Wife: "I would too. I'd like to eat out at a nice restaurant. How about you?"

Husband: "I think that's a good idea. I'd like to go to . . ."

The *under-responsible* person doesn't speak for himself, doesn't let others know what he wants or feels (or tries not to, anyway). He says things in indirect ways, often making

154

sweeping generalizations about what "everyone" thinks or feels:

"Some wives would be angry at your staying out all night."

"Other guys expect their wives to look good when they go out together."

This type of person is trying to avoid being candid about his own thoughts, feelings, and intentions. Often he is put in the position of denying his own thoughts, feelings, and intentions, almost as if he were a nonperson.

Wife: "Some wives would be angry at your staying out all night."

Husband: "You mad or something?"

Wife: "Oh no, I'm not. But some wives would be."

Another type of person, the *over-responsible* person, also leaves out the "I." But his problem is trying to speak for the other person instead of for himself. So he says what the other person thinks or feels or intends. To do this, he usually sends "you messages":

"You don't like that kind of TV program."

"You're pretty tired tonight, aren't you?"

"You want to go on a fishing trip this year, don't you?"

When you presume to speak for someone else, you proclaim that you are an expert on what he thinks, feels, or intends. You tell him that you *know* what is going on in his mind—maybe even better than he does. But can you really?

A close variation of speaking for yourself is what is called the "I message." It is very helpful in resolving conflicts. "I messages" are messages that identify where the speaker is and thus are more oriented to the speaker than to the listener. The speaker may want to modify the behavior of another person, to change a situation, or simply identify his position or feeling. An "I message" is distinguished from a "you message" in that the speaker claims the problem as his own. For example, instead of saying "*You* make me so mad" an "I message" would be, "*I* feel very angry when you do that."

An "I message" consists of three parts: the feeling, the situation, and how it affects the sender. It is a statement of fact rather than an evaluation and, therefore, is less likely to lower the other person's self-esteem. It is also less likely to provoke resistance, anger, or resentment and is, therefore, less likely to hurt the relationship. The "I message" is risky because it may reveal the humanness of the speaker and the listener may use this vulnerability against the speaker. But it helps a person to get in closer touch with his own feelings and needs. It models honesty and openness.

2. *Documenting with descriptive behavioral data.* Documenting is *describing:*

"I *think* you're elated. I see a smile on your face, and your voice sounds lyrical to me."

Documenting is an important skill. First, it increases your own understanding of yourself. It gives you a better idea of *how* you arrived at your own thoughts, feelings, and intentions. And at the same time, it gives the other person a much clearer idea of *what* you are responding to.

3. *Making feeling statements.* When you make a feeling statement, you don't know how the other person will respond. So, feeling statements are risky.

Wife: "I feel sick to my stomach when I see you bow and scrape to your boss."

There are four main ways to describe feelings verbally:

(1) Identify or name the feeling. "I feel angry"; "I feel sad"; "I feel good about you."

(2) Use similes and metaphors. We do not always have enough labels to describe our emotions, so we sometimes invent what we call similes and metaphors to describe feelings. "I felt squelched"; "I felt like a cool breeze going through the air."

(3) Report the type of action your feelings urge you to do. "I feel like hugging you"; "I wish I could hit you."

(4) Use figures of speech, such as, "The sun is smiling on

me today"; "I feel like a dark cloud is following me around today."

4. *Making intention statements* is a way of expressing your immediate goals or desires in a situation. These statements provide a different kind of self-information to the other person—an overview of what you are willing to do.

Wife: "I *want* very much to end this argument."

Husband: "I didn't know that. I thought you were too mad to stop."[5]

Here is a suggested plan of action or sequence to follow in a discussion with your spouse. This plan may help you truly resolve conflicts.

When a conflict arises, instead of demanding that you be heard, *listen carefully to the other person.* "He who returns evil for good, evil will not depart from his house" (Prov. 17:13, *NASB*). "This you know, my beloved brethren. But let every one be quick to hear, slow to speak and slow to anger" (Jas. 1:19, *NASB*). Any changes that one person wants to see in another must be heard and understood.

John Lavender suggests a method of increasing our listening and understanding capacity. This method works for many.

"A little game that can help you . . . is called RDS, or the Revolving Discussion Sequence. It's a communications game designed to help you and your mate arrive at a compromise in which no one wins at the expense of the other person's losing. The rules of the game are simple.

"One of you makes a statement. Before the other person can reply, he or she must restate, to the first person's satisfaction, what the first person said. When you have established a clear understanding that what the first person said is what the second person heard, the second person must find a way to agree with that. If there is total agreement, you don't have a problem. However, you may not agree entirely with what your mate said, so you reply in a manner such as this: 'I can agree there's considerable truth in what you say.' Or, you may grudgingly admit, 'There's a grain of truth there.' If you don't agree at all, you simply agree that this is how your mate thinks and affirm his or her right to that opinion.

"After the statement, restatement and agreement, the second person is free to make his or her statement. Again, before the mate can reply, he or she must restate, to the satisfaction of the second person, what that person said and find a way to agree with it. This process is continued until the matter is resolved.

"So the rules are simple: statement, restatement and agreement . . . statement, restatement and agreement. Hence the name: Revolving Discussion Sequence."[6]

*Select an appropriate time.* "A man has joy in making an apt answer, and a word spoken at the right moment, how good it is" (Prov. 15:23, *AMP*).

*Define the problem.* How do you define the problem and how does the other person? You could suggest that you both stop talking and write down exactly what it is that you are trying to resolve.

*Define the areas of agreement and disagreement in the conflict.* Share with the other person first of all what you agree with him about, and then ask what he disagrees with you about. Writing the areas of agreement and disagreement on paper helps clarify the situation.

Here comes the difficult part. A few conflicts may be just one-sided, but most involve contributions from both sides. *Identify your own contribution to the problem.* When you accept some responsibility for a problem, the other sees a willingness to cooperate and will probably be much more open to the discussion.

*The next step is to state positively what behaviors on your part would probably help, and be willing to ask for his opinion.* As he shares with you, be open to his feelings, observations, and suggestions. Watch out for defensiveness!

Consider the following passages from *The Living Bible:*

"If you refuse criticism you will end in poverty and disgrace; if you accept criticism you are on the road to fame" (Prov. 13:18).

"Don't refuse to accept criticism; get all the help you can" (Prov. 23:12).

"It is a badge of honor to accept valid criticism" (Prov. 25:12).

"A man who refuses to admit his mistakes can never be successful. But if he confesses and forsakes them, he gets another chance" (Prov. 28:13).

## WHAT'S YOUR PLAN?

1. Which of the conflicts in your marriage do you feel you are primarily responsible for?

2. What could you do at this time to assist in resolving these conflicts?

3. How will the presence of Jesus Christ in your life help you resolve conflicts?

4. What one conflict will you commit yourself to resolve this next week?

As you consider resolving conflicts, think upon these passages:

"Call to Me, and I will answer you, and I will tell you great and mighty things, which you do not know" (Jer. 33:3, *NASB*).

"Trust in the Lord with all your heart,

And do not lean on your own understanding.

In all your ways acknowledge Him,

And He will make your paths straight.

Do not be wise in your own eyes;

Fear the Lord and turn away from evil" (Prov. 3:5–7, *NASB*).

## Notes

1. David and Vera Mace, *We Can Have Better Marriages if We Really Want Them* (Nashville: Abingdon, 1974), p. 89.
2. *Ibid.*
3. Roy W. Fairchild, *Christians in Families* (Atlanta: John Knox Press, 1964), pp. 169, 170.
4. Some of these principles were derived from a process called Basic Emotional Communication (BEC) and are described in Carl Goldberg, *Therapeutic Partnership* (New York: Spring, 1977), pp. 139–142.
5. *Minnesota Couples Communication Program Handbook* (Minneapolis: Minnesota Couples Communication Program, 1972), pp. 23, 31.
6. John Allan Lavender, *Your Marriage Needs Three Love Affairs* (Denver, CO: Accent Books, 1978), pp. 118, 119.

## CHAPTER TWELVE

# LEARNING TO FORGIVE COMPLETELY

"When we got married, no one could have predicted what would happen in the next few years. I guess no one knows what will happen; if they did, fewer people would marry. I guess I still have hope because of my Christian faith. I just pray that we will find a way to turn back to the Lord and let His love and forgiveness heal the wounds and scars of our marriage. Forgiveness—that's a hard word. I wish someone had taught us more about that before we married. That's a word we're just beginning to learn about."

If you love another person you must be willing to run the risk of being hurt. Hurt brings pain, but through hurt comes the opportunity for forgiveness and reconciliation. Is forgiveness easy for you? Is it available to you? Have you experienced the process of forgiving others and being forgiven?

Many marriages are gradually eroded and eventually destroyed because one person is unable to forgive. A person who continually brings up something his spouse did or said in the past that was hurtful to himself continues to punish the other person and erects a wall of difference and coldness.

If we know Jesus Christ as Saviour, we have experienced God's forgiveness. Because we are in Christ, we have the capacity to forgive ourselves and thus are enabled to forgive others. Paul spoke to us directly on this account: "Be gentle and forbearing with one another and, if one has a difference (a grievance or complaint) against another, readily pardoning each other; even as the Lord has freely forgiven you, so must you also [forgive]" (Col. 3:13, *AMP*).

More than any other people, Christians have the capacity to forgive. What is forgiveness? What is it not? Perhaps one of the best ways to discover what forgiveness is, is to consider what it is not. Forgiveness is not forgetting. God constructed us in such a way that our brain is like a giant computer. Whatever has happened to us is stored in our memory. The remembrance will always be with us.

There are, however, two different ways of remembering. One is to recall the offense or hurt in such a way that it continues to affect us and our relationship with another. It continues to eat away and bother us so that the hurt remains. Another way of remembering, however, simply says, "Yes, that happened. I know it did, but it no longer affects me. It's a fact of history, yet has no emotional significance or effect. It's there, but we are progressing onward at this time, and I am not hindered nor is our relationship hurt by that event." This is, in a sense, forgetting. The fact remains, but it no longer entangles us in its tentacles of control.

Forgiveness is not pretending. You cannot ignore the fact that an event occurred. Wishing it never happened will not make it go away. What has been done is done, and becoming a martyr and pretending ignorance of the event does not help the relationship. In fact, your lack of confrontation and reconciliation may encourage the other person to continue or repeat the same act or behavior.

Forgiveness is not a feeling. It is a clear and logical action on your part. It is not a soothing, comforting, overwhelming emotional response that erases the fact from your memory forever.

Forgiveness is not bringing up the past. It is so easy to bring up past offenses and hurts. There are some who have a trading stamp book with unlimited pages. For each hurt, they lick a stamp and paste it in. When the right time comes, they cash in those pages. Bringing up the past is destructive because:

- There is nothing you can do to change it.
- It takes you away from giving your energy to the present and future.
- It makes you responsible at this point for jeopardizing the marriage.
- Even if you were severely offended, by dwelling on the offense you place a continuing burden on your marriage.
- It denies your partner the opportunity to change for the better. This behavior also denies the presence and power of the person of Jesus Christ in a life!
- It does little to elevate you in the eyes of others.

An indication of maturity is the desire and willingness to break loose of the past and move forward.

Forgiveness is not demanding change before we forgive. If we demand a change or demand proof of it first, we expose our own faithlessness and unwillingness to believe in the other person. He has already changed in a sense by coming and asking for forgiveness. The change is in his heart, but do we really trust that change?

Often, instead of complete forgiveness, we say, "I'll have to wait and see" or "Give me time." Time is often involved because forgiveness is a process and often does not occur instantaneously. We have to work through our feelings. But are we working through our feelings by ourself or waiting for definite signs of change on the part of the other person?

We don't want to risk being hurt again, so we are cautious and untrusting. This approach puts us in the role of a judge. The other person's change of heart has to be proved to us, and maybe our criteria of proof is so subjective that he can never measure up.

When forgiveness is lacking a strange bedfellow by the name of bitterness creeps in. Another word for bitterness is poison. It is poison to the person possessing it and to the relationship. The Word of God says, 'Let there be no more bitterness' (see Eph. 4:31). Bitterness means that we have the desire to get even. But getting even costs. It can cost us in our bodies—ulcerative colitis, toxic goiter, high blood pressure, ulcers. These are just a few of the by-products.

Forgiveness is rare because it is hard. It will cost you love and pride. To forgive means giving up defending yourself. It means not allowing the other person to pay. It repudiates revenge and does not demand its rights. Perhaps we could say that it involves suffering.

"Forgiving is self-giving with no self-seeking. It gives love where the enemy expects hatred. It gives freedom where the enemy deserves punishment. It gives understanding where the enemy anticipates anger and revenge. Forgiveness refuses to seek its own advantage. It gives back to the other person his freedom and his future."[1]

Forgiveness is costly and is substitutional. "All forgiveness, human and divine, is in the very nature of the case vicarious, substitutional, and this is one of the most valuable views my mind has ever entertained. No one ever really forgives another, except he hears the penalty of the other's sin against him."[2]

Our greatest example of forgiveness is the cross of Jesus Christ. God chose the cross as the way of reconciliation. "For you have been called for this purpose, since Christ also suffered for you, leaving you an example for you to follow in His steps" (1 Pet. 2:21, *NASB*). "He himself bore our sins . . . on the tree" (1 Pet. 2:24, *RSV*). And we are called to forgive as God has forgiven us. "Be as ready to forgive others as God for Christ's sake has forgiven you" (Eph. 4:32, *Phillips*).

"Forgiveness takes place when love accepts—deliberately—the hurts and abrasions of life and drops all charges against the other person. Forgiveness is accepting the other when both of you know he or she has done something quite unacceptable.

"Forgiveness is smiling silent love to your partner when the justifications for keeping an insult or injury alive are on the tip of your tongue, yet you swallow them. Not because you have to, to keep peace, but because you want to, to make peace.

"Forgiveness is not acceptance given 'on condition' that the other become acceptable. Forgiveness is given freely. Out of the keen awareness that the forgiver also has a need of constant forgiveness, daily.

"Forgiveness exercises God's strength to love and receives the other person without any assurance of complete restitution and making of amends.

"Forgiveness is a relationship between equals who recognize their need of each other, share and share alike. Each needs the other's forgiveness. Each needs the other's acceptance. Each needs the other. And so, before God, each drops all charges, refuses all self-justification, and forgives. And forgives. Seventy times seven. As Jesus said."[3]

## WHAT DO YOU THINK?

1. Describe a time when you offended another and experienced forgiveness. What was your inner response or feeling?

2. Describe how you feel when you forgive another.

3. When is it hardest for you to forgive?

4. What would be the most difficult thing to forgive your spouse for?

5. What is it like to you to know that God forgives you?

---

Forgiveness involves other elements as well. Healing is a part of this process. It is not patching up. Patch-up jobs are partial jobs. Healing means restoration and a bringing back to full health. Healing also means that when we remember what has occurred, we remember the reconciliation rather than the hurt. When a person comes to you for forgiveness, he is aware of the hurt he has caused in your life. That hurt is the reason for seeking forgiveness. Perhaps the person coming to you and seeking forgiveness is saying something like this:

"I know that a tremendous loneliness (or anger or insecurity or fearfulness) is going on inside you because of my failure to be present to you, to take you into consideration and to live my life with you in mind." I ask you to take your eyes off the hurt and focus on our relationship, and to say, '*We* are more important than the hurt.'

"When I am seeking forgiveness I am most aware, not of what I have done, but of what is going on inside you. If I look at what has been done to me, then I'm going to estimate it in terms of right and wrong and of how serious it is. But there's no need to even consider that, for when I say, 'Please forgive me,' I have already recognized the evil involved in my actions. I'm not defending myself at all, and though I'm certainly not bypassing what I have done, I'm focusing on something more important—what is going on inside you, the one who will be doing and forgiving."[4]

An example of two fathers from the Word of God can best demonstrate what forgiveness is and what it is not. The first

166

example is found in 2 Samuel 13–18. This is the story of Absalom and David. Absalom's sister Tamar was raped by her half-brother Amnon. Absalom hated his half-brother for this act, plotted against him, and then had him killed by his servants. And David mourned for his son. Absalom fled and stayed away for some time. "So Absalom fled to Geshur, and was there three years; and the Spirit of King David longed to go forth to Absalom, for he was comforted about Amnon, seeing he was dead" (13:38,39, *AMP*).

Eventually David was confronted about bringing his son back, and he told Joab to bring back his son. "So Joab arose, went to Geshur, and brought Absalom to Jerusalem. And the king said, Let him go to his own house, and let him not see my face. So Absalom went to his own house, and did not see the king's face" (14:23,24). "Absalom dwelt two full years in Jerusalem, and did not see the king's face" (14:28, *AMP*).

Here we have an example of unexpressed affection on the part of David for his son as well as incomplete forgiveness. There was not a complete restoration, and the results were tragic. Eventually Absalom led a revolt against David, and Joab's armor-bearers killed him. When David heard of Absalom's death, his remorse was deep. "And the king was deeply moved, and went up to the chamber over the gate, and wept; and as he went, he said, O my son Absalom, my son, my son Absalom! Would God I had died for you, O Absalom, my son, my son!" (18:33, *AMP*). Because David's forgiveness of Absalom was incomplete—it was limited and conditional—David lost his son.

In Luke 15 we have a positive example of forgiveness in the account of the prodigal son and the forgiving father. After the son had his fill of living away from home, having squandered his money, he came to his senses and decided to go home. The account goes like this:

"But when he came to his senses, he said, 'How many of my father's hired men have more than enough bread, but I am dying here with hunger! I will get up and go to my father, and will say to him, "Father, I have sinned against heaven, and in your sight; I am no longer worthy to be called your son; make me as one of your hired men." ' And he got up and came to his father. But while he was still a long way off, his father saw him, and felt compassion for him, and ran and embraced him, and kissed him. And the son said to him, 'Father, I have sinned against heaven and in your sight; I am no longer worthy to be called your son.' But the father said to his slaves, 'Quickly bring out the best robe and put it on him, and put a ring on his hand and sandals on his feet; and bring the fattened calf, kill it, and let us eat and be merry; for this son of mine was dead, and has come to life again; he was lost, and has been found.' And they began to be merry" (Luke 15:17–24, *NASB*).

Here, the father expressed open affection and complete forgiveness. He didn't wait to see if his son would crawl to him. He got up and went to his son. He celebrated his return and restored him fully to his position. There were no conditions, no "proving" time. It was a time of rejoicing. Does this happen in your life when you experience confession and forgiveness? It is possible, because Christ has set us free to forgive others.

**WHAT DO YOU THINK?**

1. How can you fully express to another that you forgive him?


2. Can you think of a person in your life right now who really needs your forgiveness?


3. What can you do at this time? What would you say to this person?

What if you are the person who needs to confess and forgive at this time? What can or should you do? Confession is turning ourself over to another. And there is a difference between saying "I'm sorry" and "Will you forgive me?" *Forgive* and *sorry* express two different experiences. Being sorry recognizes that what you did was not right, but you may have some justifying excuse for it. In asking forgiveness, the emphasis shifts from you to the other person. Your relationship is not right because of you. In asking forgiveness, you don't give excuses. It is not easy; it is difficult and it costs.

Experience forgiveness with this couple: "One night Dick said everything he could to hurt Sherry. She was bewildered and anguished.

"He was concerned all the next day. What was Sherry going to say when he got home? More important, what was he going to say? This wasn't something he could pretend hadn't happened. He knew he couldn't just walk in and be especially nice. He was going to have to face himself and Sherry.

"When Dick walked through the door he saw that Sherry's eyes were red and puffy. She stiffened as he went to hold her and she turned away. Dick held on to her and gently turned her face so that he could look into her eyes. 'Honey, last night I was ugly. Saying I'm sorry just doesn't cover that. I want you to forgive me. I need your forgiveness to make me whole again.'

"The film disappeared from Sherry's eyes, her muscles gradually unwound as she leaned against him and held him tight. Tears of relief welled up in her eyes and after a few moments she whispered, 'I forgive you.'

"Later, Sherry said, 'Thanks for doing that. I was all set for a stormy session. I was going to make you see how horribly you had treated me. When you asked me to forgive you my heart stopped. I quit thinking about how bad you were and began to realize I wasn't perfect either. Who was I to grant forgiveness? You were sincere and put yourself in my hands. I will never forget it. I believe forgiveness has to be the greatest moment of closeness two human beings can ever have!' "[5]

Louis H. Evans, Sr., added this thought about forgiveness:

"An apology is so often considered a sign of weakness, whereas in reality it is a sign of strength. It is more difficult, sometimes, to confess our weaknesses or to parade our faults in the face of those whom we most dearly love than in the presence of anyone else. This may be a recoiling from any chance of destroying the other's respect for us. It may also simply be ego in its proudest parade."[6]

Forgiveness involves choosing to change our actions and attitude. We have to risk being open and vulnerable. We say we are willing to change our present direction. We cannot place any demands upon the other person. We cannot say, "I'll confess to this if you promise that you won't get upset or hold it against me." We must take the risk.

What is it that we confess? Everything? Are there guidelines? David Augsburger suggested the following guidelines:

"If a man repents, that is, honestly and completely turns away from his past and its sins, must he confess it all? Certainly confession will bring a tremendous release and relief for his tortured feelings of guilt. But what then? Will she be able to forgive, forget and accept him again? Will the confession be constructive, bringing healing and health once more to their relationship? Or will it be a block that nothing will be able to remove for her? Will it embed hostilities in her soul that she is not emotionally, spiritually and mentally able to overcome? Will it be constructive or destructive of love, understanding and acceptance?

"Then when and where should confession be made?

"Confession should be as public as the commission of the act. Only those directly involved should be told in your confession. Sin should not be published for general public consumption and speculation.

"Confession should be shared where it is a help to another,

170

not a hurt or a hindrance. If confessing your sin would provide another with excuses or tempt him to stumble, don't!

"Confession should not be so intimate, so revealing, so painful that it will wound or scar the person to whom it is confessed. Such careless, thoughtless confession to a close friend or lover may bring you release, but it will transfer the painful burden to the other. Do you want to be healed at the expense of another's suffering?"[7]

Over the years, we have found what you might call a handle that opens the door to forgiveness and makes it both easier and possible. That handle is prayer—not just individual prayer but praying together as a couple. The prayer life of a couple is the quality cement that adds a lasting adhesiveness to a couple's relationship. The closeness and emotional intimacy that are demanded and that occur as a result of praying together will make forgiving one another a natural part of the marriage relationship. Consider these thoughts about prayer:

"It is only when a husband and wife pray together before God that they find the secret of true harmony, that the difference in their temperaments, their ideas, and their tastes enriches their home instead of endangering it. There will be no further question of one imposing his will on the other, or of the other giving in for the sake of peace. Instead, they will together seek God's will, which alone will ensure that each will be fully able to develop his personality. . . . When each of the marriage partners seeks quietly before God to see his own faults, recognizes his sin, and asks the forgiveness of the other, marital problems are no more. Each learns to speak the other's language, and to meet him halfway, so to speak. Each holds back those harsh little words which one is apt to utter when one is right, but which are said in order to injure. Most of all, a couple rediscovers complete mutual confidence, because, in meditating in prayer together, they learn to become absolutely honest with each other. . . . This is the price to be paid if partners very different from each other are to combine their gifts instead of setting them against each other."[8]

"Forgive, and forget the past. Dwelling on past hurts, bringing up past faults, or limiting one's present acts by expecting a repetition of past behavior only builds up emotional barriers. How easy it is to 'imprison' your partner mentally in a certain pattern of behavior, thereby condemning him to remain unchanged. Our faith is in a God who can and does work miracles, both in ourselves and in others.

"In prayer, forgive your spouse for whatever has happened. Go even further and accept responsibility for all the misunderstandings that have grown up between the two of you. Needless to say, your partner cannot receive your forgiveness unless he repents. God forgives you, even before you sin, so practice forgiveness toward your spouse regardless of attitudes you may feel justified in expecting from him."[9]

### WHAT'S YOUR PLAN?

1. Do you pray together as a couple with openness and honesty?

2. If not, what will it take to start a prayer life together?

3. How often and how much time would you like to spend in prayer with your spouse?

4. If you feel a need to offer forgiveness to your spouse for a lingering hurt, take a piece of paper and write a personal, constructive letter to him to help you formulate your thoughts.

5. If you feel that you have offended your spouse in any way, write a letter asking for his forgiveness and sharing your love with him.

## Notes

1. David Augsburger, *70x7: The Spirit of Forgiveness* (Chicago: Moody Press, 1970), p. 40.
2. James O. Buswell, Jr., *A Systematic Theology of Christian Religion* (Grand Rapids: Zondervan, 1962), 2:76.
3. David Augsburger, *Cherishable Love and Marriage* (Harrisonburg, VA: Herald Press, 1976), p. 146.
4. Chuck Gallagher, *Love Is a Couple* (New York: William H. Sadlier, 1976), pp. 128, 129.
5. Gallagher, p. 125.
6. Louis H. Evans, *Your Marriage—Duel or Duet?* (Old Tappan, NJ: Fleming H. Revell, 1975), pp. 98, 99.
7. Augsburger, *70x7*, pp. 67,68.
8. Paul Tournier, *The Healing of Persons* (New York: Harper & Row, 1965), pp. 88, 89.
9. Lionel Whiston, *Are You Fun to Live With?* (Waco, TX: Word Books, 1968), p. 116.